W9-ATN-597

THE LUCENT LIBRARY OF
SCIENCE AND TECHNOLOGY

The Search for Extraterrestrial Life

by Don Nardo

LUCENT BOOKS

An imprint of Thomson Gale, a part of The Thomson Corporation

THOMSON

GALE

Detroit • New York • San Francisco • San Diego • New Haven, Conn. • Waterville, Maine • London • Munich

LIBRARY OF CONGRESS CATALOGING-IN-PUBLICATION DATA

Nardo, Don, 1947–
  The search for extraterrestrial life / by Don Nardo.
    p. cm. — (The Lucent library of science and technology)
  Includes bibliographical references and index.
  ISBN 1-59018-832-2 (lib. bdg. : alk. paper) 1. Life on the other planets—Juvenile
literature. I. Title. II. Series.
QB54.N3725 2006
576.8'39—dc22

                                                    2005017877

Printed in the United States of America

TABLE OF CONTENTS

FOREWORD

"The world has changed far more in the past 100 years than in any other century in history. The reason is not political or economic, but technological—technologies that flowed directly from advances in basic science."

— Stephen Hawking, "A Brief History of Relativity," *Time,* 2000

The twentieth-century scientific and technological revolution that British physicist Stephen Hawking describes in the above quote has transformed virtually every aspect of human life at an unprecedented pace. Inventions unimaginable a century ago have not only become commonplace but are now considered necessities of daily life. As science historian James Burke writes, "We live surrounded by objects and systems that we take for granted, but which profoundly affect the way we behave, think, work, play, and in general conduct our lives."

For example, in just one hundred years, transportation systems have dramatically changed. In 1900 the first gasoline-powered motorcar had just been introduced, and only 144 miles (232km) of U.S. roads were hard-surfaced. Horse-drawn trolleys still filled the streets of American cities. The airplane had yet to be invented. Today 217 million vehicles speed along 4 million miles (6,437,376km) of U.S. roads. Humans have flown to the moon and commercial aircraft are capable of transporting passengers across the Atlantic Ocean in less than three hours.

The transformation of communications has been just as dramatic. In 1900 most Americans lived and worked on farms without electricity or mail delivery. Few people had ever heard a radio or spoken on a telephone. A hundred years later, 98 percent of American homes have telephones and televisions and more than 50 percent have personal computers. Some families even have more than one television and computer, and cell phones are now commonplace, even among the young. Data beamed from communication satellites routinely predict global weather conditions, and fiber-optic cable, e-mail, and the Internet have made worldwide telecommunication instantaneous.

Perhaps the most striking measure of scientific and technological change can be seen in medicine and public health. At the beginning of the twentieth century, the average American life span was forty-seven years. By the end of the century the average life span was approaching eighty years, thanks to advances in medicine including the development of vaccines and antibiotics, the discovery of powerful diagnostic tools such as X-rays, the lifesaving technology of cardiac and neonatal care, improvements in nutrition, and the control of infectious disease.

Rapid change is likely to continue throughout the twenty-first century as science reveals more about physical and biological processes such as global warming, viral replication, and electrical conductivity, and as people apply that new knowledge to personal decisions and government policy. Already, for example, an international treaty calls for immediate reductions in industrial and automobile emissions in response to studies that show a potentially dangerous rise in global temperatures is caused by human activity. Taking an active role in determining the direction of future changes depends on education; people must understand the possible uses of scientific research and the effects of the technology that surrounds them.

The Lucent Books Library of Science and Technology profiles key innovations and discoveries that have transformed the modern world.

Each title strives to make a complex scientific discovery, technology, or phenomenon understandable and relevant to the reader. Because scientific discovery is rarely straightforward, each title explains the dead ends, fortunate accidents, and basic scientific methods by which the research into the subject proceeded. And every book examines the practical applications of an invention, branch of science, or scientific principle in industry, public health, and personal life, as well as potential future uses and effects based on ongoing research. Fully documented quotations, annotated bibliographies that include both print and electronic sources, glossaries, indexes, and technical illustrations are among the supplemental features designed to point researchers to further exploration of the subject.

The Beginning of True Understanding?

"Either we are alone in the universe or we are not," commented President Richard Nixon's science adviser, Lee DuBridge. "Either way, it's mind-boggling."[1] This now famous statement beautifully sums up a basic reality of humanity's ongoing search for extraterrestrial life—life that may exist beyond Earth. On the one hand, the discovery of such life would be exciting, awe-inspiring, and humbling. It would show that humans and other Earth creatures make up only a tiny part of a greater whole, one that stretches for unimaginable distances into unknown reaches of a vast universe. On the other hand, finding out that humanity is alone in all that vastness would be equally jolting and humbling. It would mean that we have a special birthright. If so, we would have an equally special responsibility to nurture our unique gift of life and be a wise, constructive sole steward of the cosmic domain.

As for the central question underlying DuBridge's statement, philosophers and political leaders, along with the public at large, have answered it differently at various times in history. The ancients almost

Among the trillions of stars that exist in the universe, are humans alone or merely one of many intelligent races?

unanimously accepted the existence of other inhabited worlds. "There is an infinite number of worlds, some like this world, others unlike it,"[2] advocated the fourth-century B.C. Greek philosopher Epicurus. His contemporary, the Greek thinker Metrodorus, concurred: "To consider the Earth as the only populated world in infinite space is as absurd as to assert that in an entire field of millet, only one grain will grow."[3]

These men were convinced that divine forces would not be so wasteful as to create an entire world and leave it empty and useless.

The pendulum of thought on the subject swung the other way in the Middle Ages, however. Western society came to be dominated and guided by the Roman Catholic Church, which firmly rejected the idea of other inhabited worlds. Church leaders told their flocks that Earth and, by extension, humanity were the center of God's creation. According to this view, all natural elements and bodies moved around or toward Earth. As astronomer Steven J. Dick points out:

> For Christianity, a plurality of worlds directly confronted its omnipotent God. For suppose God wished to create another world. How could he do so given the principle . . . that if there were more than one world, the elements . . . would have more than one natural place toward which to move, a physical and logical contradiction.[4]

In modern times the pendulum of thought regarding extraterrestrial life swung again. Today, the notion that life on other worlds may exist is widely accepted. Increasing numbers of scientists have come around to this view (though a significant minority is still doubtful). And a number of polls taken in the 1990s revealed that a majority of people in the United States and Europe believe that there is some kind of life beyond Earth.

THE SCIENTIFIC COMMUNITY ENERGIZED

Until recently, this belief had to be taken almost completely on faith. The chances that life developed on other worlds in the solar system (the Sun and all the planets and other bodies that orbit it) seemed remote. And no hard evidence had ever been found for the existence of extrasolar planets (planets orbiting other stars).

These views changed rather suddenly, however, in the last few years of the twentieth century. Spacecraft sent to study the giant planet Jupiter revealed that several of its larger moons have oceans of water beneath their icy surfaces. And where there is water, there may be life, a number of researchers pointed out. Also, in 1995 scientists discovered the first known extrasolar planet. Many more were found in the years that followed and the number, now well over a hundred, continues to grow.

These and other related discoveries have greatly energized the scientific community to increase its efforts to search for extraterrestrial life, both in our own solar system and beyond. Efforts to examine the Sun's water worlds are in the planning stages. And hundreds of professional scientists and thousands of amateurs are presently involved in researches collectively called SETI—the Search for Extraterrestrial

This is an image from SETI's "at home" program, which utilizes the home computers of thousands of volunteers.

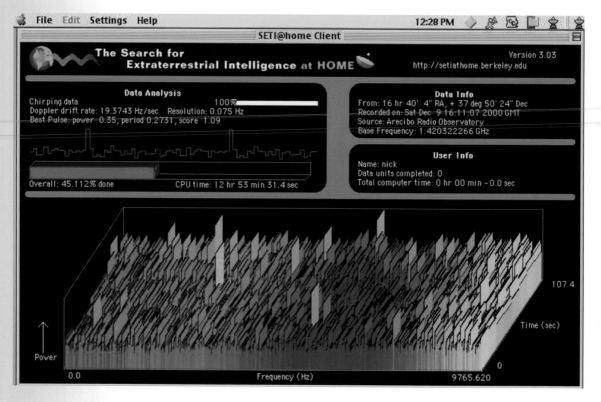

Intelligence. SETI's main goal is to detect long-range alien signals and thereby prove the existence of life on other worlds. The ultimate objective, of course, is not merely to detect such signals, but to establish direct communication with such beings, if they do indeed exist. The most optimistic members of the scientific community go a step further and imagine the day when humans and aliens might find some way to bridge the immense distances that separate them and meet face-to-face.

TO UNDERSTAND OURSELVES

All this optimism and energy concerning the possibility that humanity is not alone has found a kind of central meeting of the minds in the form of an emerging new scientific field. As researchers David Koerner and Simon LeVay put it:

> Experts in many diverse disciplines have come together to forge a new science: astrobiology, exobiology, cosmic biology—call it what you will—it is a fundamentally new enterprise, a focus of intense excitement and energy, and a recipient of huge government resources. This science has just one ambition: To understand life in its universal context, and in doing so, to understand ourselves.[5]

Indeed, if and when the existence of extraterrestrial life is confirmed, one of its most valuable immediate lessons will be to show humanity some basic realities about itself. "Faced with intelligent creatures from another world, creatures who look nothing like us," says noted science writer Ben Bova, "we will at last recognize that all humans are brothers and sisters, that each of us is part of the same family. That moment will mark the end of humankind's adolescence and the beginning of true understanding."[6]

CHAPTER 1

Hunting for Earth-Like Planets

Ultimately, the search for extraterrestrial life may take humanity on a mind-bending journey through the far, unknown reaches of outer space. Yet that exciting quest must invariably begin in a more familiar and seemingly mundane place—Earth. That is because thus far our planet is the only place in the universe where it can be proven that life did develop. By examining how life came to be on Earth, scientists hope to gain insight into how this process might have occurred elsewhere in the depths of space.

One of the most basic facts about Earth is that life appeared on our planet when it was still quite young. Studies of ancient rocks show that Earth formed roughly 4.5 billion years ago, and simple one-celled creatures already existed 3.8 billion years ago. Moreover, these primitive life-forms developed under extremely harsh physical circumstances. During its first few hundred million years, Earth was constantly bombarded by asteroids, comets, and other space debris. Their impacts created an ever-changing landscape rocked by unimaginable violence. Also, thousands of volcanoes spewed huge quantities of poisonous gases into the planet's primordial atmosphere. Scientists postulate that primitive life may have begun to develop several times, but could not survive in the harsh conditions.

No sooner had the period of major bombardment and volcanism subsided, however, than life did take hold in Earth's emerging oceans. So presumably, many scientists say, simple life-forms could well have established themselves on young planets orbiting other stars. Scientists also make the assumption that the young planets in question are Earth-like. That is, they are about the size of Earth, have rocky surfaces punctuated by bodies of liquid water, and lie at appropriate distances from their parent stars. If a planet is too close to a star, for instance, conditions on that planet will be too hot to support life, and if it lies too far from the star, conditions will be too cold. The planet must exist, therefore, in a region around the parent star that has temperatures and other conditions friendly enough to support the growth of some kind of life. Scientists call such friendly regions around stars habitable zones.

Of course, all of these factors pertaining to extrasolar planets presuppose the existence of such planets in the first place—whether they are Earth-like or not. Indeed, for a long time no one knew for sure if other stars had planets.

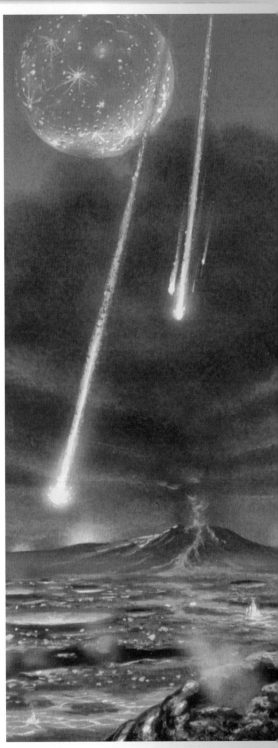

When Earth was young, most of its surface was hot, molten, and constantly changing, conditions that were inhospitable to life.

Astronomers and interested laymen alike long considered their existence highly probable, but concrete proof was lacking. Then, quite suddenly, scientists began to detect extrasolar planets. Between 1995 and 2005, scientists found more than 120 planets orbiting 105 stars. Naturally, high on the list of the researchers' concerns was how many of these planets are Earth-like and therefore at least capable of supporting life.

A MOMENTOUS DISCOVERY

That they would actually find themselves examining and measuring alien planets came as a pleasant surprise to modern astronomers. Many of them did not expect to find proof of extrasolar planets in their lifetimes. This is partly because Earth-based telescopes are not powerful enough to directly detect the images of objects so faint and so close to stars. Even the Hubble Space Telescope, which has the advantage of operating above the distorting effects of Earth's atmosphere, cannot see and photograph extrasolar planets. On the one hand, planets are very small in comparison to stars, so the light that extrasolar planets reflect toward Earth is extremely faint. Making matters worse, the light from a parent star typically drowns out the feeble light from its planets. As a result, astronomers had to be content with the hope that extrasolar planets *might* be detected by future telescopes large enough to do the job.

The momentous discovery of the first alien planet was unexpected, therefore, and in fact occurred quite by accident. In October 1995, two Swiss astronomers, Michael Meyor and Didier Queloz, were searching for stellar companions. Scientists had long known that many stars are binary, meaning that they travel in pairs, each companion held in the other's embrace by their combined gravities. The stars in some binary systems are about the same size, so both are easily visible in telescopes.

But often one stellar companion is very small and faint, forcing astronomers to use other means to detect it. The most common technique analyzes light from the visible companion to reveal how it moves through space. This technique is possible because light waves act very much like sound waves.

Michael Meyor and Didier Queloz hold the issue of Nature *in which they published their discovery of the first extrasolar planet.*

The pitch of sound waves increases as the waves approach a listener and decreases as they move away from the listener. A familiar example is the rising and falling sound of an ambulance siren as the vehicle passes by. In 1848, an Austrian physicist named Christian Doppler determined that light waves act in a similar manner. When a beam of light approaches an observer, the light's spectrum, or rainbow of colors making up the beam, shifts toward the blue end. In contrast, when the light beam is moving away, the spectrum shifts toward the red end. Thanks to this so-called Doppler effect, Ben Bova points out, "slight shifts in a star's spectrum can tell astronomers whether the star is moving toward or away from us."[7]

Meyor and Queloz used the Doppler effect to study a Sun-like star called 51 Pegasi (named for Pegasus,

Pictured is an artist's conception of the planet 51 Pegasi B orbiting its parent star, 51 Pegasi.

the flying horse, the constellation in which the star lies in the night sky). They hoped that the star would appear to wobble slightly as it moved along. That would reveal that a small, visually undetectable companion star was pulling it to and fro.

These astronomers did detect a wobble in 51 Pegasi's motion. But to their surprise, it was far too tiny to be caused by even a very small star. That meant the companion must be a planet. The existence of this extrasolar planet, the first ever found, was quickly confirmed by other astronomers.

Further studies revealed that 51 Pegasi B, as astronomers dubbed the planet, has about half the mass of Jupiter, the largest planet in the Sun's family. That makes the new planet about 160 times heftier than Earth. 51 Pegasi B also lies very close to its parent star. It is so close, in fact, that it takes only four days to move around the star, so a year on 51 Pegasi B is only four days long! (In comparison, Mercury, the closest planet to the Sun, orbits in 88 days and Earth orbits in 365 days.) Another consequence of the new planet's close proximity to its parent star is a great deal of heat. Surface temperatures on 51 Pegasi B reach as high as 2,500°F (950°C), near the melting point of cast iron. Clearly, then, the first extrasolar planet discovered is not Earth-like.

REALMS OF GIANTS AND "ROASTERS"

Still, the discovery of 51 Pegasi B did provide firm proof that the planets in our solar system are not unique. In the months and years that followed, many more extrasolar planets were found. Among the newest was one confirmed in January 2003 that has an orbital period of only 1.2 days, making its year even shorter than that of 51 Pegasi B. At the other extreme, astronomers have found a planet that takes a full fifteen years to orbit its star (as compared to Jupiter, which orbits the Sun in about thirteen years).

The extrasolar planets discovered to date also show a wide range of sizes. The largest has seventeen times the mass of Jupiter (about forty-three hundred times Earth's mass) and the smallest is about a tenth the size of Jupiter (about thirty-two times bigger than Earth). Despite their great contrast in size, therefore, all of these planets are a good deal larger than Earth.

Another characteristic that most of the new planets have in common is that they do not lie where scientists had expected giant planets to exist. In our solar system, the giant planets—Jupiter, Saturn, Uranus, and Neptune—lie in the middle to outer regions of the Sun's family. The rocky "terrestrial" planets—Earth, Mars, Venus, and Mercury—lie much closer to the Sun. It was long assumed that this general arrangement would be the norm in star systems.

But the systems observed so far do not have this arrangement. Most of the extrasolar giants, like 51 Pegasi B, lie very close to their parent stars. This makes them so hot that scientists have given them the nickname "roasters." One notable exception, discovered in the summer of 2003, is a planet that orbits HD70642, a faint star located about ninety light-years from the Sun. (A light-year is the distance light travels in a year, or about 6 trillion miles [9.654 trillion km].) This planet is about the size of Jupiter and moves around HD70642 in a circular orbit very similar in size to that of Jupiter.

DO JUPITERS MAKE EARTHS POSSIBLE?

Astronomers continue to find extrasolar planets in increasing numbers. Because most of those discovered to date are roasters, as well as giants (which are probably mainly gaseous in form), conditions on them are too inhospitable to support life as we know it. An animal or human being who visited one of these planets would first collapse and be crushed to death by its huge gravity. The remains would then

SOME EXTRASOLAR PLANETS

Planets orbiting other stars (not our own Sun) are called extrasolar planets. For a long time, no one knew for sure whether other stars had planets. But between 1995 and 2005, scientists discovered more than 120 extrasolar planets orbiting 105 stars. In the next step in the search for extraterrestrial life, researchers must determine how many of these planets are Earth-like and capable of supporting life.

Planet Name	Parent Star	Constellation	Size of Planet [1]	Year Discovered	Discovered by	Star's Distance from our Sun [2]
51 Pegasi b	Pegasi B	Pegasus	0.47	1995	Michael Meyor and Didier Queloz, Geneva Observatory, Switzerland	48 light-years
70 Virginis b	70 Virginis	Virgo	6.60	1996	San Francisco State University Planet Search	59 light-years
HD 70642 b	HD 70642	Puppis	2.00	2003	Anglo-Australian Telescope, Australia	94.5 light-years
TrES-1	GSC 02652-01324	***	0.75	2004	Trans-Atlantic Exoplanet Survey (TrES), a network of small telescopes in the United States and Europe	500 light-years
HD 117207 b	HD 117207	Centaurus	2.06	2005	Keck Observatory, Hawaii	107 light-years

1. Mass of planet measured in relation to Jupiter size, where Jupiter = 1.
2. One light-year equals 5,865,696,000,000 miles (9,460,800,000,000 kilometers).

Source: NASA-JPL PlanetQuest (http://planetquest.jpl.nasa.gov).

be cooked and charred by the searing heat. Scientists agree that it is highly unlikely that life could have developed on these planets in the first place.

However, many astronomers hope that smaller, rocky planets like Earth and Mars may exist in some of these distant systems. Such Earth-like planets may be particularly likely to exist in systems like that of HD70642, in which the gas giants lie in orbits similar to those in the Sun's system. These alien terrestrial planets, scientists say, may simply be too tiny to detect using the technology presently available.

Moreover, evidence suggests that the very fact that Jupiter-like planets are so common may be a sign that Earth-like planets are common, too.

MAJOR REQUIREMENTS FOR PLANET FORMATION

Recent studies of stars in the neighborhood of the Sun and beyond show the major requirements that appear to be necessary for planets to form around them. Noted science writer Robert Zimmerman explains in this excerpt from an article in the August 2004 issue of *Astronomy*:

It appears . . . that the more massive a star, the more likely it will have planets. Type M dwarf stars, with masses a tenth to a third the Sun's mass, almost never have planets . . . while G stars, like our Sun, have planets some 7 percent of the time. And F stars, 30 to 50 percent more massive than the Sun, have planets about ten percent of the time. Furthermore, single stars seem to form planets more often than binary systems do. . . . Finally, a star's composition seems important. Right from the beginning, scientists noticed that extrasolar planets are more likely to orbit stars that are at least as rich in complex atoms as our Sun. These heavier atoms, which astronomers broadly term "metals," are the result of several episodes of star formation, with each new generation of stars adding its own heavier atoms to the star-making mix.

In recent years scientists have run complex computer simulations of the formation of solar systems. These tests show that small, rocky, Earth-like planets commonly accompany larger gas giants. After a star forms, giant gaseous planets form out of a big disk of gases, dust, and debris swirling around the star. Planetesimals, the mountain-sized building blocks of smaller, rocky planets, then form from the remaining debris. At first the planetesimals remain in circular orbits around the star and do not grow much more. But then the gravity of one or more Jupiter-sized planets causes these planetesimals to fall out of orbit and collide and form larger objects. In this way, in the words of science writer Tim Appenzeller, "Jupiters help Earths take shape."[8] What is more, the Jupiters in the various systems likely later act as guards for the smaller planets. The giants absorb most of the impacts from the largest stray asteroids and comets, increasing the chances for the terrestrial planets to have long, stable lives.

HOW MANY EARTH-LIKE PLANETS?

If these simulations and estimates are roughly correct, Earth-like planets are probably fairly common in the universe. How many are likely to exist in our galaxy, the Milky Way? (A galaxy is an enormous mass of stars held together by their mutual gravities.) First, consider that the Milky Way is made up of at least 100 billion stars. All of the extrasolar planets discovered so far exist in the Sun's immediate neighborhood, a very tiny portion of the galaxy as a whole. The fact that so many stars in a small, selected region have planetary systems suggests that large numbers of stars in other parts of the Milky Way will also have them.

To be on the conservative side, however, let us suppose that only 10 percent of stars in the galaxy have planetary systems. Now suppose that only 20 percent of these systems have just one Earth-like planet. Even using these low estimates, the number of Earth-like planets in the Milky Way is still huge—in the range of 2 billion.

This spiral galaxy, which lies millions of light-years away from Earth, closely resembles our own Milky Way.

That number multiplies many times when one travels out beyond our galaxy. One of the Milky Way's neighbors, the Andromeda Galaxy, has 200 billion or more stars, a few billion of which likely have Earth-like planets. Moreover, untold billions of other galaxies exist, stretching all the way to the farthest limits that human telescopes can see. Therefore, the universe probably contains many trillions of Earth-like planets. Not all of these planets necessarily harbor life. But remember that life developed on Earth under highly adverse conditions. So it is far from a stretch of believability to suggest that the same thing occurred on at least some of the other Earth-like worlds.

A PROMISING FUTURE

Scientists are confident that they will be able to begin directly detecting these terrestrial planets in the near future. In 2007, NASA will launch the Kepler Mission (named for Johannes Kepler, an early astronomer). It will consist of a space telescope that will seek out extrasolar planets in an ingenious way. Sometimes the planets Mercury and Venus pass across the Sun's disk as seen from Earth. During such transits, some of the Sun's light is blocked. The Kepler device will search for such transits around distant stars and measure the approximate sizes of the transiting bodies by the amount of light they block. "If Earth-sized planets are common," scientists Seth Shostak and Alex Barnett say, "the mission will find at least some of them."[9]

Even more promising is the Terrestrial Planet Finder (TPF), which NASA plans to launch sometime between 2014 and 2020. This large space telescope will be specially designed to blot out the bright light of parent stars, making their planets directly visible. The TPF will be so sophisticated that it will be able to do simple analyses of distant planetary atmospheres. If a faraway planet "has an atmosphere like ours,"

KEPLER'S UNBLINKING GAZE

NASA is presently in the planning stages of the Kepler Mission, designed to search for extrasolar planets by observing transits of planets across the disks of distant stars. When a planet passes in front of a star (as seen from Earth), the star's light dims a little. The sophisticated telescope aboard the Kepler craft will be able to measure the amount of dimming in such cases. And this measurement will give scientists an estimate for the size of the transiting planet. Kepler is scheduled to spend at least four years monitoring the brightness of some eighty thousand stars located in the constellation of Cygnus (the swan). If the telescope detects a dimming event, it will look at the same star two more times to confirm it. Scientists involved in the project say that three dimming events in a row will constitute proof of the presence of an extrasolar planet.

A NASA illustration shows what the Kepler Space Telescope will look like in orbit.

Appenzeller says, "TPF should be able to see signs such as carbon dioxide and water vapor. If the atmosphere is rich in oxygen . . . TPF should detect it." These gases may be signs of life. If and when humans detect them, they will be "a first hint that the universe may not be as lonely a place as it has seemed."[10]

CHAPTER 2

Exploring the Sun's Water Worlds

In confirming the existence of extrasolar planets, scientists have taken a major step in the search for possible extraterrestrial life. This statement is based on the reasonable assumption that, to take hold and grow more complex, primitive life-forms need the hospitable conditions provided by certain planetary environments. One of the most obvious of these conditions is temperature. The presence of various elements and chemicals needed to create living tissues is also essential, as is some form of energy source to activate living organisms.

But perhaps the most crucial condition for the development of life, most scientists believe, is the existence of at least moderate quantities of liquid water. No one knows yet the exact manner that life began on Earth. But it is fairly certain that the process in which inorganic, or nonliving, materials transformed into organic ones took place in the planet's early oceans and/or tidal pools. Water became the solvent or lubricant, so to speak, that allowed the earliest organic materials to organize themselves and thrive. "Life, when you get right down to it, is chemistry," Seth Shostak and Alex Barnett point out.

And chemistry consists of reactions between various compounds. If organic compounds are floating in a liquid (such as happens within a living cell), they can more easily meet and react. A cell without liquid would be like a party where everyone was forced to sit in a chair all night, unable to drift around the room. Social contacts would be limited. In addition to encouraging reactions, liquids are also useful for bringing food to cells, and for carrying waste products away. So a fluid is required to keep cells functioning and is presumably also necessary to get the molecules of life together in the first place.[11]

When Earth is viewed from space, its most prominent feature consists of its oceans of liquid water.

This basic connection between life, at least as we know it, and water partly accounts for why complex life-forms evolved on Earth. Our planet lies more or less in the middle of the Sun's habitable zone, the relatively warm region where liquid water can exist on planetary surfaces. Indeed, Earth, with some three-quarters of its surface covered by water, is the chief water world in the Sun's family.

Only a few years ago, astronomers assumed that Earth was the *only* planet in the solar system that ever had any appreciable amounts of water. However, recent discoveries suggest that Mars, though not a true water planet now, once possessed abundant water. (Mars does lie in the outer reaches of the Sun's habitable zone.) Moreover, in the last decades of the twentieth century, space probes revealed that several of the moons of the giant planets have water oceans beneath their icy surfaces. These discoveries have opened up what many experts view as thrilling new possibilities for finding evidence of extraterrestrial life in our own cosmic backyard.

WATER ON MARS?

The revelation that Mars may once have had oceans of water has particularly excited scientists. After all, Mars has long been the most popular candidate for life beyond Earth, both in scientific circles and in science fiction literature and movies. In the late 1800s, a few astronomers claimed they saw canals criss-crossing Mars's surface. This led to a popular notion among members of the general public (though not among most scientists) that intelligent Martians had constructed these waterways. H.G. Wells and other popular fiction writers then took the idea a step further and depicted Martians traveling to and attempting to conquer Earth. The "invaders from Mars" theme was repeated so often that the term *Martian* became more or less synonymous with the terms *alien* and *extraterrestrial*.

Eventually, NASA probes revealed what most as-tronomers had long suspected—the Martian canals had been optical illusions. Mars's surface clearly possessed neither water nor any sort of civilization. But initial photos taken from Mars's orbit showed something that took most scientists by surprise. Many of the planet's surface features look as though they had been created by flowing water, including what might be dried-up riverbeds.

Other indications of former water on Mars were provided by a later probe—the *Mars Global Surveyor*, which achieved orbit around the red planet in 1997. The probe showed strong evidence of erosion caused by water flowing on or just beneath the surface, perhaps as little as 100,000 years ago. This discovery led astronomers to propose that some water may still exist in a frozen state beneath Mars's surface. Perhaps, they say, occasional warming trends on the planet melt the ice, releasing brief flash floods that carve out telltale surface features.

These gullies in the wall of a crater on Mars were cut in the distant past by flowing water.

It should be noted that a few scientists think these features were not caused by water. It may be, they say, that Mars has little water, in which case the riverbeds and erosion were caused by liquid carbon dioxide (CO_2) that may form in high-pressure conditions underground. However, most planetary scientists remain optimistic that fair amounts of water ice will eventually be found on Mars. If so, they will make that planet a strong candidate for the development of life, even if only the most primitive variety.

ARE WE MARTIANS?

So far, none of the Earth probes that have landed on Mars's surface and analyzed the dirt and rocks have found any firm evidence for any sort of life. However, that does not necessarily mean that the planet is lifeless. Some scientists point out the possibility that basic life-forms developed on a wetter Mars long ago and that some of them may still linger in or near pockets of water or water ice in various places beneath the surface. They note that some hardy forms of bacteria and other primitive creatures have been found living in darkness and under enormous pressures nearly 2 miles (3.2km) beneath Earth's surface.

Another possibility, of course, is that some time after life developed in Mars's ancient oceans, it was destroyed by a natural catastrophe. A strike by an asteroid or comet, similar to but larger than the one now believed to have wiped out the dinosaurs on Earth, could easily have eradicated all Martian life. But this scenario raises another intriguing possibility. When such cosmic impacts occur on planets (or their moons), rocks and other debris are blasted from the surface. Most of these objects eventually succumb to gravity and fall back, but a few continue on into space. Over time, they can make their way to other planets, whose gravities pull them in. To date, scientists have found thirty-two meteorites on Earth that originated on Mars.

These particular Mars rocks are only a few million years old and devoid of life. But the process that brought them to Earth has presumably been going on for billions of years. In fact, it must have occurred much more frequently in the solar system's early years, when planetary bombardments were more frequent. Some scientists say it is possible that primitive Martian life-forms developed in Mars's oceans and then made their way to Earth's early oceans by hitching rides on meteorites. Science writer Alan Longstaff reports:

> Calculations by planetary scientists give good reason to believe some microorganisms could survive . . . a lengthy journey through interplanetary space, provided they were surrounded by about a yard of rock to shield them from cosmic radiation. . . . Terrestrial bacteria have survived . . . the vacuum and cold of space for over two years, and their spores can spend perhaps millions of years in suspended animation.[12]

Thus, the possibility, even if it is remote, exists that the primitive life-forms that took hold in Earth's primordial oceans were not natives, but came originally from another water planet—Mars.

Rocks carrying primitive life-forms may have long ago blasted off the surface of Mars and crashed on Earth.

ICE VOLCANOES IN SATURN'S REALM?

Even if no life ever developed on Mars when it possessed flowing liquid water, the solar system features several other water worlds providing potential habitats for living things. The newest known water world is Enceladus, one of Saturn's many moons. This moon has long piqued the interest of astronomers because it is unusually bright for its size (318 miles [512km] across), which means that its surface is highly reflective. In the early months of 2005, NASA's *Cassini* spacecraft flew by Enceladus, which had never before been studied up close. Mission scientists were astonished to find that it has an atmosphere because the tiny object lacks the gravity to hold onto gases for very long. The only explanation was that Enceladus's atmosphere is constantly being replenished from somewhere. But where?

The answer was provided by *Cassini*'s analyses of Enceladus's atmosphere and surface. The "air" on the moon is made up of water vapor and the surface is composed almost entirely of water ice. "That raises the intriguing possibility that ice volcanoes or geysers spew gases from the moon's interior," says *Astronomy* magazine's Richard Talcott.

> Such eruptions could explain the Saturnian moon's brightness. As water blasts out, bigger droplets would freeze and fall back to the surface, coating it with a bright patina of fresh ice. . . . Tides seem the only plausible source for the heat needed to drive such geological activity. Saturn's immense gravity raises a tidal bulge in Enceladus . . . [which] continually flexes and heats its interior.[13]

Scientists do not yet know how much liquid water exists inside Enceladus. There may not be enough to form an ocean, and even if there is, other

No Undersea Civilizations?

If living creatures have indeed developed in the dark inner seas of Europa and other icy worlds of the outer solar system, could some of them have become intelligent enough to create a civilization? Most scientists say this is unlikely. In their book *Cosmic Company*, astronomers Seth Shostak and Alex Barnett explain why:

> Would a massive marine alien be smart? Some biologists claim that the ocean isn't a very challenging environment. The weather's the same from day to day, and as a swimmer you don't have to climb hills or maneuver around rocks. They suggest that this situation might forever fail to encourage great intelligence in sea creatures. . . . But even if sophisticated sea dwellers exist, it's unlikely that they would develop science and technology. Industrial processes—for example the fabrication of raw materials—would be difficult in salt water. Ocean inhabitants might never discover the stars . . . or for that matter invent radio communication (most radio waves don't penetrate water). So even if there are smart submersible aliens, it is unlikely that we will ever find them with our SETI experiments.

requirements for the creation of life may not be present. Future missions to this bizarre little world will hopefully shed some light on these mysteries.

Life in Europa's Dark Depths?

In the meantime, scientists are more certain about the existence of extensive oceans inside several other moons in the outer solar system. Regarding the potential for life, the most promising of these is Europa, one of Jupiter's four largest natural satellites. The first indication that Europa might have an interior ocean was provided by photos taken by *Voyagers 1* and *2*, NASA probes that flew near Jupiter and its moons in 1979. Another NASA craft, *Galileo*, which reached Jupiter in 1995, snapped much more detailed photos and confirmed the existence of large amounts of water inside Europa.

POTENTIAL WATER WORLDS

Planets must possess at least moderate quantities of liquid water for life-forms to develop and live. Unmanned spacecraft have provided enough data on these moons to theorize that they may contain at least some liquid water below their icy surfaces. Future visits to these worlds may give scientists enough additional information to make a determination regarding their suitability for life.

Name of Moon	A Satellite of...	Diameter*	Possible Water Features
Enceladus	Saturn	311 miles (500 kilometers)	Scientists know that Enceladus's surface is almost completely covered with water ice. Volcanoes or geysers may heat water to liquid form below the icy crust. Scientists will require more information to determine how much liquid water may exist on this moon.
Europa	Jupiter	1,945 miles (3,130 kilometers)	Above its rocky mantle and under an outer layer of ice is probably a layer of water thirty to sixty miles deep—water totaling about twice the volume of all of Earth's oceans combined. Geothermal heat from the moon's core may provide enough heat for plants or other organisms to exist in Europa's dark waters.
Ganymede	Jupiter	3,280 miles (5,262 kilometers)	The surface of Ganymede, the largest moon in our solar system, consists of a crust of rock and a thick layer of water ice. Below this rock and ice may be a mantle of ice and liquid water, perhaps even an ocean up to three miles deep.
Callisto	Jupiter	2,985 miles (4,800 kilometers)	Callisto's makeup is uncertain, but NASA believes the moon may have a large icy mantle. It may also contain a salt-water ocean of undetermined depth.

* For comparison, Earth's diameter equals 7,926 miles (12,756 kilometers), and our moon measures 2,160 miles (3,476 kilometers) across.

Sources: NASA Solar System Exploration (http://solarsystem.nasa.gov), and NASA Planetary Fact Sheets (http://nssdc.gsfc.nasa.gov/planetary/planetfact.html).

The moon's surface "is woven with a complex patchwork of fractures, ridges, bands, and spots," science writer Robert Pappalardo explains.

From the complex pattern of markings on the moon, planetary scientists can deduce how Europa has been molded. . . . Galileo's gravity measurements indicate Europa probably has [a] layer of H_2O about 60 miles (100km) thick above a thick, rocky mantle and a central, iron-rich core. . . . If most of the water layer is liquid, its volume would be twice that of all Earth's oceans combined.[14]

Scientists would like to know if life has somehow taken hold in the dark depths of Europa's sea. If it has, they realize, its formation required some sort of input from a powerful energy source. On Earth, the chief energy source supporting life is the Sun, which has bathed our planet in a warm bath of its light for billions of years. Almost no sunlight makes it through Europa's outer layer of ice, however. So if life does exist on that moon, it was helped along by some other energy source. One possibility is the heavy doses of radiation that Europa regularly receives from its parent, Jupiter.

The more likely major energy source on Europa, though, is geothermal heat—abundant warmth radiating up from Europa's warm core. This might have contributed to the formation of life similar to several strange organisms recently discovered living in total darkness around small volcanic vents at the bottoms of Earth's oceans. Among these are one-celled creatures known as lithoautotrophic microbes. For nutrients, these bizarre critters absorb carbon and nitrogen from various substances that filter down from the oceans' upper layers. Does this significant discovery "open the door for subsurface ecologies on other worlds?" asks Gerald A. Soffen, of NASA's Goddard Space Flight Center.

One thing to remember is that many of these vent-dwellers do not require sunlight. Their energy is derived from chemical reactions. . . . This has profound implications for life on places such as . . . Europa, where the surface is covered with ice but the interior may be warm enough to allow life-sustaining liquid water.[15]

Earth's history has shown that where single-celled creatures arise, multicelled ones are likely to develop, too. So a growing number of astronomers are hopeful that future exploratory expeditions to Europa will reveal a wide range of aquatic plants and animals similar in some ways to those that exist in Earth's seas.

EXPEDITIONS TO THE WATER WORLDS

Such expeditions will not limit themselves to exploring Europa. Planetary scientists strongly suspect that oceans of liquid water lie beneath the icy shells of two of Jupiter's other large moons—Ganymede and Callisto. Indeed, Ganymede, the largest moon in the solar system at 3,270 miles (5,260km) in diameter, may have an interior ocean 3 miles (4.8km) deep. And Callisto "almost certainly contains an ocean of salty water,"[16] Pappalardo reports.

NASA's first planned mission to explore Jupiter's water worlds was mounted in 1998 but was canceled in 2002 due to budgetary problems. However, another expedition has since taken shape and is expected to launch in about the year 2015. The *Jupiter Icy Moons Orbiter*, or JIMO for short, will, at a minimum, visit Europa, Ganymede, and Callisto.

In addition to taking photos while orbiting these moons, JIMO will launch probes designed to explore Europa's (and perhaps Ganymede's) mysterious inner seas. Scientists at the Jet Propulsion Laboratory at the California Institute of Technology are presently constructing these unique probes. (They were originally conceived to explore the depths of Lake Vostok, which lies under the Antarctic ice sheet, but are being modified for use in the outer solar system.) Dubbed "cryobots," each is about three feet long and looks something like a torpedo. During the mission, JIMO will drop a cryobot onto Europa's surface and warm water in the probe's nose will begin melting the ice, causing the device to sink deeper and deeper.

SCIENTIFIC FINDS STIMULATE THE IMAGINATION

In recent years the possibility that living creatures might have developed in the depths of Europa's seas has inspired a number of scientists and others to write fictional works speculating about such life. The most outstanding example is Arthur C. Clarke's great novel *2010: Odyssey Two*. In the story, a race of superintelligent and very powerful extraterrestrials detects primitive creatures struggling to survive in the dark waters beneath Europa's surface. The advanced aliens put the Europans on the road to higher intelligence by stimulating the development of their mental abilities. Then, to ensure that humans do not interfere, the advanced aliens forbid Earth ships from approaching or landing on Europa. In the intriguing finale of the story, which takes place twenty thousand years in the future, the cosmic experiment is revealed to be a success. Most of Europa's icy shell has melted, and the Europans have emerged onto the land, where they are building towns and beginning to ponder the wonders of the universe.

Life may exist beneath Europa's strange, fractured surface. But could it be intelligent?

When the sinking cryobot finally enters Europa's interior sea, onboard lights will flick on and various cameras and detectors will search for life.

No one knows what these devices will discover in those strange, dark depths. Perhaps these distant seas will prove to be devoid of life. If life *is* found in them, however—even primitive life—the discovery will be monumental. As Pappalardo says, it will be nothing less than a "revolution in our understanding of the universe not experienced on this planet since Galileo turned his telescope skyward and first spied these moons."[17]

Chapter 3

Seeking the Building Blocks of Life

It has been established that the existence of liquid water is one of the crucial requirements for the development of life on a planet (or moon or other cosmic body). Some sort of energy source—sunlight or geothermal heat, for example—is another requirement. Also important are the basic building blocks of life, which are suspended in the water and acted on by the energy sources. These building blocks consist of atoms and molecules of common elements that exist not only on Earth but throughout the universe. When these atoms and molecules combine in appropriate ways, they form the tissues and vital organs of living things.

For biologists and other scientists, the central question relating to the formation of life has always been this: Which elements are most basic and essential to its structure and survival? On one level, oxygen is certainly essential to Earthly animal life, since all animals need to breathe oxygen to live. But on a more fundamental level, the tissues of both animals and plants are composed of a different element—carbon. In fact, all life on Earth is based on, or structured around, chemical compounds in which

THE IMPORTANCE OF CARBON

Carbon is abundant in the universe, and it is one of the most common elements on Earth. All life on Earth is based on chemical compounds in which carbon atoms predominate. Most scientists believe that life on any other planet in our universe will be similarly carbon-based.

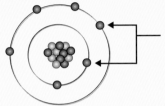

The carbon atom contains six electrons—two orbit the nucleus in the inner shell, and four in the outer shell.

The carbon atom is unique in that it can join together with other carbon atoms in many different ways. Here are a few examples of those carbon-only molecule structures:

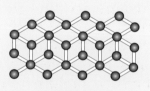

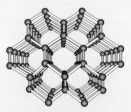

Graphite
Atoms combine in hexagon-shaped rings on one plane. Graphite is used in pencils; it is one of the softest minerals on Earth.

Diamond
Atoms combine into a three-dimensional structure; the bonds are very difficult to break. Diamonds are one of the hardest minerals on Earth.

Fullerene
Atoms combine in a spherical or tube-shaped structure.

Carbon atoms are very versatile and easily combine with atoms of other elements to form many important compounds. Ten million different carbon compounds are known to exist, and thousands of these are important to life processes.

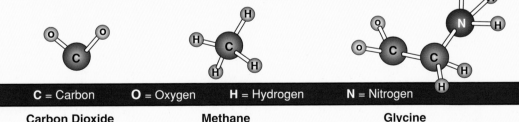

C = Carbon   **O** = Oxygen   **H** = Hydrogen   **N** = Nitrogen

Carbon Dioxide
Carbon dioxide is essential to the existence of plant life.

Methane
One of many hydrocarbons, methane is a type of fossil fuel used for energy.

Glycine
Amino acids such as this simple one combine with other amino acids to form proteins, essential to cells of humans and other life-forms.

carbon atoms predominate. The main reason that this single element can give rise to so many different kinds of living things is that it is very versatile. As Ben Bova explains:

> Carbon atoms can join together to form ladders, rings, tubes, spirals, and springs, as well as chains of different lengths. Carbon-based molecules can absorb light or emit light. . . . They can be endothermic (heat-absorbing) or exothermic (heat-releasing). . . . Organic chemistry, the chemistry of life, is all about carbon-chain molecules. Since carbon is also one of the most abundant elements in the universe, biologists and astronomers interested in extraterrestrial life have concluded that carbon-based life should be the most common form everywhere, and carbon-based life is what we should look for.[18]

If these assumptions about carbon and life in the universe are true, a certain amount of carbon will need to exist on a planet or other cosmic body as a prerequisite of life. "A planet that has little carbon cannot sustain a viable biosphere [environment in which life exists]," scientist Alan E. Rubin points out. On the other hand, he says, "a planet that has an overabundance of carbon will have a thick atmosphere rich in carbon dioxide, stifling surface temperatures"[19] and making the survival of life impossible. To have life as we know it, therefore, carbon must be abundant, but not too abundant, in a given environment.

But what about life as we do *not* know it? Some scientists caution that it may be premature to decide that carbon compounds are the only chemical route to life. They propose that one or more other elements might, under the right conditions, lead to the formation of living things. In their view, those who insist on the carbon route may be biased by their experience with Earth life, which may not be the norm for universal life.

LIFE ON TITAN?

Interactions of carbon compounds with other elements and water may not be the only type of organic chemistry in the universe, some scientists speculate. In fact, one possible alternate process might be at work right now in our own solar system. Saturn's largest moon, Titan, has a thick atmosphere, about 50 percent thicker than Earth's, in fact. Titan's air is composed mainly of nitrogen, methane, and lesser amounts of hydrocarbons such as ethane (an ingredient of gasoline) and propane.

The *Huygens* spacecraft (a joint venture of NASA and the European Space Agency) landed on Titan on January 14, 2005. Before shutting down from the numbing cold, the probe confirmed that liquid methane exists in large quantities on the moon's surface. Water also exists on Titan, though in a frozen state. Some scientists say it is possible that the methane could act as the chief solvent in a chemistry in which hydrocarbons become increasingly complex, driven in part by heat generated from Titan's interior. More sophisticated missions to the moon will be needed before the existence of such an exotic organic chemistry can be confirmed.

The surface of Titan, Saturn's largest moon, may contain pools of liquid methane.

CARBON HERE, THERE, AND EVERYWHERE?

Whether it is the only route to life or one of several, carbon is certainly plentiful in many parts of the solar system and presumably in other star systems. In addition to the abundance of carbon and carbon compounds on Earth, carbon-chain molecules were detected by the *Galileo* probe in Jupiter's atmosphere. These molecules are not themselves alive. But when placed in suitable conditions—an ocean of water and sufficient heat or other energy sources, for instance—perhaps they could become the building blocks of life, as happened on Earth. Some scientists

The intense colors of the Martian surface and sky are captured by a camera on one of NASA's Viking *Landers.*

have suggested that abundant water might lie deep beneath Jupiter's turbulent outer cloud layers. "If a planet-wide ocean of water really exists beneath Jupiter's clouds," one researcher writes,

> it could be the site of great biological activity. Perhaps the organic molecules that the Galileo probe discovered in Jupiter's clouds rain down on that world-spanning ocean like manna from heaven. Perhaps complex organisms swim in that vast sea and feed on them.[20]

Abundant quantities of carbon have also been found on the surfaces of many of Jupiter's moons, as well as on some of Saturn's and Uranus's moons. And studies have shown that carbon compounds exist in comets. Comets are hunks of ice, rock, and dust that many astronomers liken to "dirty snowballs." Most orbit the Sun in a shell of debris called the Oort Cloud, which lies well beyond the orbits of the outermost planets. But on occasion comets drift into the inner solar system, where they grow tails and are sometimes visible with the naked eye from Earth. More important, comets sometimes strike our planet. One prevailing theory is that many of the carbon compounds and much of the water that gave rise to life on Earth came from comets. If so, it is possible that comets have seeded other planets, both in the Sun's family and beyond, with life-giving materials.

So far, scientists have not been able to test cometary materials in labs on Earth to see the exact composition of their carbon compounds. However, NASA probes *have* analyzed the soil of Mars. In July and September 1976, the *Viking Landers* reached the surface of the red planet. Robotic arms scooped up soil samples and tested them in miniature onboard labs. No organic molecules—that is, particles made up of carbon compounds—were found in these experiments. But a number of experts are not discouraged.

They say that high doses of ultraviolet rays from the Sun, which strike Mars during its daylight hours, would destroy most or all carbon-chain molecules. It is possible, they say, that organic molecules might exist well beneath the Martian surface, where Earth probes cannot detect them.

CARBON COMPOUNDS FROM MARS

Ironically, one intriguing piece of evidence for carbon-based organic molecules on Mars comes from a piece of that planet found on Earth. One of the thirty-two known Mars rocks, dubbed ALH 84001, was found in Antarctica, where it landed roughly thirteen thousand years ago. Researchers are sure that the rock came from Mars because traces of gases trapped inside it exactly match the Martian atmosphere, which the *Viking Landers* measured with extreme precision in the 1970s.

But it was something else lurking inside the meteorite that really caught the attention of scientists. Microscopic studies revealed tiny fossilized (stone-like) shapes that strongly resemble living and fossil Earth bacteria. In addition, researchers found what appear to be small globules (spheres) of carbonates, compounds composed of carbon and oxygen. Carbonates are regularly made by Earth bacteria. Moreover, inside the carbonate globules were molecules of a specialized class of carbon compounds, called polycyclic aromatic hydrocarbons (PAHs), which living things on Earth give off when they decay. "Put these points together," Bova says, "and you have a picture of bacterial life existing underground on Mars some 3.5 billion years ago, similar to the time when life was getting started on Earth."[21]

A number of scientists disagree with this conclusion, however. They say it is possible that the so-called fossilized bacteria inside ALH 84001 are just mineral grains that look like bacteria. In their view, the carbonates and PAHs in the meteorite might

This microscopic view of the Martian rock ALH 84001 shows the fossil-like rods and globes suspected of being artifacts of life.

have been deposited there by unknown processes. The scientific community is still undecided, therefore, whether these Martian carbon compounds are the product of life.

PIECING TOGETHER THE BUILDING BLOCKS

Even if the carbon molecules and globules found inside ALH 84001 are not artifacts of living organisms, carbon-based life might well have evolved on other Earth- and Mars-like planets in the universe. To formulate a general idea of how this process may have taken place, scientists have intensely studied the only examples of life available—those on Earth. In a very real way, Earth life has become a yardstick, or model, for the development of extraterrestrial life. The scientists involved in this research do not rashly assume that life elsewhere in the universe will be identical to life on Earth. But they do make the general assumption that certain basic chemicals and physical conditions must exist anywhere for life to get started.

On Earth, the substances and physical conditions that started life on its way existed when the young planet was still in a chaotic, violent state. Asteroids, comets, and even larger cosmic objects bombarded Earth, constantly reshaping its surface. And the atmosphere was made up of poisonous gases, many of them vented by hundreds of volcanoes erupting simultaneously.

Some people find it difficult to believe that living things could develop in such nightmarish conditions. But that is in fact what happened. To shed light on exactly how, beginning in the 1950s scientists attempted to reproduce in labs the conditions on the early Earth. Their immediate goal was to find out if organic substances can develop from inorganic ones under such conditions. In particular, they wanted to see if very complex carbon compounds—amino acids—could form because amino acids are the building blocks of the proteins that make up the tissues of living things.

This photo shows Stanley Miller at work in his University of Chicago lab in 1953.

What is now viewed as the classic experiment of this type took place in 1953. Stanley Miller, a graduate student at the University of Chicago, and his professor, Harold Urey, proposed that the action of lightning, radiation, and other kinds of energy on inorganic chemicals in Earth's early seas caused the creation of the first living cells. Miller started out with a glass beaker containing a mixture of water, methane, ammonia, and hydrogen. This mixture represented Earth's early atmosphere and seas. Then Miller began zapping the elements in the container with an electric discharge, which represented the early Sun. After just a week, about a sixth of the methane in the container had been transformed into more complex molecules, including glycine and alanine, two of the simplest of the amino acids that occur in proteins. As the late, great science explainer Isaac Asimov remarked, "If this could be done in small volumes over very short periods of time, what could have been done in an entire ocean over a period of many millions of years?"[22]

In the decades that followed, many scientists repeated and enlarged on this experiment. In all cases, the results were strikingly similar—the formation of organic materials in a lab. Although no one claims that actual, full-blown life was created in this process, such experiments clearly show how the basic building blocks of life *could* have come together on the early Earth. It also follows, says astrobiologist Paul Davies, "that if this state of affairs had come about on Earth, it could also have come about on other planets, too."[23]

ALTERNATIVE CHEMISTRIES FOR LIFE

The Miller-Urey experiment and others like it concentrated on the formation of carbon compounds in a watery environment. This, after all, is the process that took place on the early Earth. But some experts have speculated that, despite carbon's great versatility, it might provide only one potential pathway to life. As researcher Clifford Pickover puts it:

> It is not necessary for an atom to bond to itself to form long chains [as carbon does]. In fact, the chains could be made of two or more atoms in alternation. . . . Life could be constructed using an alternative chemistry in which the possibilities are not as vast as those of carbon. For example, although the English language can be communicated and stored using 26 letters, it can also be coded as successfully . . . with 1s and 0s, the binary code used by computers. In the same way, a less complex chemistry could serve as the genetic basis for life.[24]

Most often mentioned as an alternative to carbon as a basis for the building blocks of life is the element silicon. On Earth, silicon is a major ingredient of rocks, sand, and glass. These substances are not alive. But living silicon-based entities would not necessarily be crystal- or rocklike, as softer tissues like those of Earth plants and animals would be perfectly possible for such beings. The main reason living tissues are pliable is that the basic building blocks are suspended in or surrounded by a liquid solvent.

The main question, therefore, is which liquid silicon-based life would use as a solvent, in the same ways that Earth life uses water as a solvent. Liquid ammonia has been cited as a possibility. This fluid boils at $-28°F$ ($-33°C$) and freezes at $-107°F$ ($-77°C$). This means that average conditions on a planet dominated by silicon-based life would need to be between -50 and $-80°F$ (-46 and $-62°C$). Scientists are confident that the universe contains plenty of planets and moons that fall into this category. Other theoretical organic chemistries feature solvents such as liquid methane or muddy "soups" of hydrocarbons. Some scientists postulate that just such an exotic chemistry might exist on Saturn's largest moon, Titan.

The possibility of creatures living in what, to humans, are poisonous liquids and freezing temperatures may at first glance seem farfetched. However, some scientists are quick to point out that living things routinely thrive in extreme, poisonous environments right here on Earth. Scientists have appropriately come to call them "extremophiles."

THE MILLER-UREY EXPERIMENT

In 1953, graduate student Stanley Miller performed a significant experiment with his University of Chicago professor, Harold Urey. Miller proposed that the action of lightning, radiation, and other kinds of energy on inorganic chemicals in Earth's early seas caused the creation of the first living cells.

Miller created a closed system using glass flasks and tubes containing water and gases.

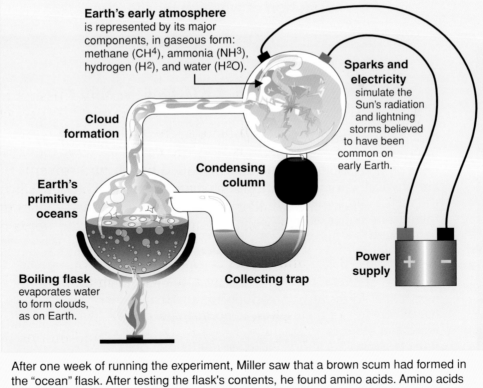

Earth's early atmosphere is represented by its major components, in gaseous form: methane (CH_4), ammonia (NH_3), hydrogen (H_2), and water (H_2O).

Cloud formation

Sparks and electricity simulate the Sun's radiation and lightning storms believed to have been common on early Earth.

Condensing column

Earth's primitive oceans

Power supply

Boiling flask evaporates water to form clouds, as on Earth.

Collecting trap

After one week of running the experiment, Miller saw that a brown scum had formed in the "ocean" flask. After testing the flask's contents, he found amino acids. Amino acids combine with other amino acids to form proteins, which are essential to human and other cellular life.

They include bacteria that flourish in industrial solvents, microbes that live in the boiling water of hot springs and under deep layers of ice, creatures that exist without oxygen (and actually find it toxic), and organisms that thrive in acids so powerful they can dissolve human skin in seconds. "Until recently," Gerald Soffen writes,

> we knew little of these exotic environments. They and the ecologies they support have been out of our convenient reach. As our studies probe further, we realize that historically we have had a very limited view of what forms life might take. Extremophiles could be the template [model] for life found on other planets. At the very least, we must be prepared to expand our notion of where to look for life.[25]

ARE HUMANS THE EXTREME ONES?

Scientists have found extremophiles living in large numbers in varied environmental niches across the globe. So it is perfectly plausible that alien creatures could exist in similar extreme conditions on other worlds. All of the extremophiles observed on Earth are physically primitive. But that probably reflects the fact that the niches they inhabit are small and largely isolated, impeding them from higher development. For example, the abundant oxygen in Earth's atmosphere would prevent the development of advanced versions of oxygen-hating microbes. But what might happen on a planet *without* oxygen (or with very little)? There, the same sort of organism might have plenty of opportunity to evolve into higher forms. It is interesting to note that sentient oxygen-haters would see themselves as normal and oxygen-loving humans and other Earth creatures as weird. "The term extremophile reflects a bias," Clifford Pickover points out (in *The Science of Aliens*). "Aliens living in environmental extremes would think we were the extremophiles."

CHAPTER 4

Weighing the Chances of Alien Intelligence

So far, the quest for extraterrestrial life in our solar system has taken for granted that such life, if it exists, will be relatively primitive. If life is indeed found someday beneath the Martian surface, for example, scientists do not expect it to be much more advanced than bacteria or simple fungi. Similar expectations exist for any life that may be found in Europa's subterranean seas. There, seaweedlike plants and fishlike animals are likely to be near the top of the evolutionary ladder. In fact, this same sort of scenario may prevail, more or less, in neighboring star systems and across the entire universe. The consensus of most scientists is that a majority of alien life-forms will consist of plantlike and animal-like species with little or no intelligence.

However, that does not rule out the existence of intelligent beings by any means. The fact is that intelligence did evolve in the universe at least once— here on Earth. This means that the development of intelligence is not impossible; therefore, it may well have occurred elsewhere, even if only rarely.

But what do scientists mean by *intelligence*? Unfortunately, this term can be imprecise and

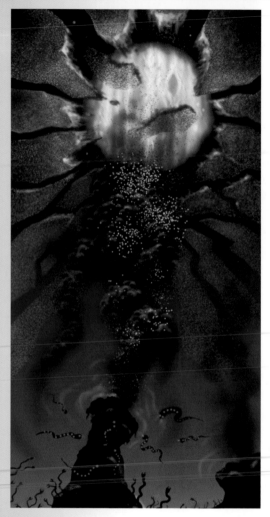

An artist envisions primitive life-forms floating around a hot geothermal vent on the floor of Europa's ocean.

misleading because it can be applied in too many relative, subjective ways. Some people argue that chimpanzees are intelligent, for example, because they can use simple tools and learn human sign language. Others say dolphins and dogs are intelligent because they can be trained to do many tasks and are capable of expressing love and loyalty. Clearly, then, there are various levels of intelligence, certainly here on Earth and perhaps on unknown numbers of alien planets. To clarify and refine the search for intelligent extraterrestrial life, therefore, a more narrow definition of intelligence is needed. In fact, when scientists discuss intelligent alien life, they usually mean sentient life. The term *sentient* means conscious and self-aware and implies the ability to use tools to construct a civilization. Thus, scientific discussions of alien intelligence inevitably consider the abilities of hypothetical extraterrestrials (ETs) to develop technology and use it to reshape their home environments and perhaps eventually to travel into space.

Once again, scientists do not need to ask if such a scenario is possible, since humans are presently using technology to reshape our planet and to explore space. A more fundamental question is how likely the development of sentience and technological civilizations is in the universe. Is it common or is it a rare occurrence? At present, no one knows the answers to these questions. Still, scientists have uncovered tantalizing clues that have inspired them to make intriguing educated guesses.

IS SENTIENCE RARE OR EVEN NONEXISTENT?

The scientific community has long been divided about the existence of extraterrestrial intelligence. On one side are those who maintain that the development of human intelligence was a chance and highly unlikely occurrence. It was the result of billions and trillions of random events, they say. And the chances that all or even most of these events would be repeated in the same order somewhere else is almost nil. The great English biologist Alfred Russel Wallace, who conceived the modern theory of evolution at the same time Charles Darwin did, made this argument. "The total chances against the evolution of man, or an equivalent moral and intellectual being, in any other planet," he wrote in 1904, "will be represented by a hundred millions of millions to one."[26]

NO ALIEN LIFE UNLESS GOD WISHES IT?

The great English biologist Alfred Russel Wallace rejected the notion of extraterrestrial life. In his 1904 book, *Man's Place in the Universe*, excerpted here, he argues that the appearance of life on Earth was too rare an event to be repeated, either on this planet or another. The one exception, he says, would be if God intervened and created alien life for his own purpose, although Wallace admits he could not fathom what that purpose might be.

The improbabilities of the independent development of man, even in one other world—and far more in thousands or millions of worlds, as usually supposed—are now shown to be so great as to approach very closely [to] impossible. Of course this whole argument applies only to those who believe that the entire material universe, inclusive of man himself, is the product of the immutable laws and forces of nature . . . the view of pure science. . . . [Others] believe that the universe is the product of mind, that it shows proofs of design, and that man is the designed outcome of it, and [suggest] that other worlds in unknown numbers have also been designed to produce man. . . . To these I reply that such a view assumes a knowledge of the Creator's purpose and mode of action which we do not possess; that we have no guide to His purposes.

The equally prominent twentieth-century biologist George Gaylord Simpson agreed. He called the immense series of random events leading to human intelligence a "causal chain of events" and asserted that if any link in that chain had been somehow different, "homo sapiens [the human species] would not exist."[27]

Those scientists who agree that the development of human intelligence was a matter of blind chance like to point out the role of mass extinctions in history. About 65 million years ago, they say, an asteroid struck Earth and wiped out more than 70 percent of all living species, including the dinosaurs. If this single, random event had not occurred, the small mammals that then existed would not have had the freedom to evolve into larger, smarter forms that eventually came to dominate the world. In short, sentient humans would never have developed.

DO BIOLOGICAL DRIVES FAVOR INTELLIGENCE?

On the opposite side of this argument are scientists who are much more optimistic about the chances for the evolution of intelligence. Given the enormous numbers of stars and planets and the abundance of organic materials in space, they think it is unlikely that life arose only once in the universe. Indeed, they say, there may exist a biological imperative, or innate universal drive, for the development of increasing intelligence and eventually, where possible, true intelligence.

If this is true, what factors may be driving this natural trend toward increasing intelligence among creatures in a given environment? On Earth, say biologists, the process in which predators hunt food and their prey try to avoid becoming that food clearly favors the survival of the smarter members of each species. "Intelligence seems to be a powerful tool for self-preservation," scientist Terence Dickinson points out.

In any particular species, the smart guys get food, while the stupid ones die off. This appears to be a fundamental rule on Earth, and it results in larger and larger brains as life evolves over broad spans of time. If we discover life on another planet, we might also expect to find that the most successful creatures on that alien world are those with the largest brains and the greatest ability to think their way out of trouble and into the next meal.[28]

Among predators, like the lion seen here, nature favors those who best use their cunning, a form of intelligence.

Increasingly complex social interactions among members of a given species may also spur the development of higher intelligence. Consider a clever male hunter that learns to share his catch with other members of his pack. If he shares food with several females, he will have a better likelihood of mating with them and passing on his genes, including those that contributed to his cleverness, to future generations. Another crucial social activity is child-rearing.

As Shostak and Barnett put it, "Animals that spend a lot of time caring for their offspring obviously reap more benefit from intelligence. Learning from your parents is valuable for survival."[29]

Another theory, called evolutionary convergence, also posits that biology is driven toward increased intelligence. Evolutionary convergence occurs when completely different kinds of creatures arrive, quite independently, at the same solution to a given problem. Flight is perhaps the most celebrated example. Various species of birds, insects, fish, mammals, and reptiles all evolved the ability to fly. In a similar manner, intelligence may develop independently on different planets in response to similar sets of physical and biological circumstances.

HOW MANY INTELLIGENT RACES?

Accepting for the moment that sentient races of ETs do sometimes evolve in the universe, how often has this happened? No one can say for sure, of course, until concrete evidence is found. But a surprisingly large number of scientists have ventured educated guesses. In the 1950s, for example, noted astronomer Sebastian von Hoerner suggested that one in 3 million stars in a given galaxy might have a planet with a race of intelligent beings. That adds up to thirty to forty thousand such planets in an average-sized galaxy. Other experts have estimated more or fewer than this number of extraterrestrial civilizations in each galaxy.

Each of these early estimates of alien races was based on a different set of criteria, since no general consensus yet existed about which criteria were most important. The beginnings of such a consensus came in what is now viewed as the most important early discussion of the subject. In 1961, a group of prominent scientists met at the National Radio Astronomy Observatory in Green Bank, West Virginia. There, astronomer Frank Drake first presented a mathematical equation that neatly included all the relevant factors connected to possible alien civilizations. It came to be called the "Drake equation" in his honor, although other scientists, most notably astronomers Carl Sagan and Ioseph (Joseph) Shklovskii, later refined it in various ways.

The relevant factors about alien civilizations addressed in Drake's equation are expressed as a series of variables. Two important variables are the number of stars in a galaxy and the estimated portion of these stars that have planets. Obviously, the higher the number of stars and planets in a galaxy, the higher the possible number of extraterrestrial civilizations. Other variables in the equation include the number of planets in each star system that bear the conditions needed for life, the fraction of these planets on which living creatures actually develop, the fraction of these creatures that evolve into intelligent beings, the fraction of these intelligent races that develop a technological civilization, and the average lifetime of such a civilization.

It is clear that the Drake equation can produce widely different results, depending on how liberal or conservative one is in estimating the various factors involved. If one believes that very few planets will give rise to life of any kind, for instance, the number of intelligent races will be small. Even by extremely conservative estimates, however, many sentient races may exist. In their classic book on the subject, *Intelligent Life in the Universe*, Sagan and Shklovskii estimated that between fifty thousand and one million intelligent races might exist in the Milky Way alone.

Astronomer Frank Drake poses next to his famous equation expressing the probabilities of ET life.

Although some astronomers think that this estimate is too high, their more optimistic opponents point to some crucial recent discoveries that directly affect some of the variables in the Drake equation. Chief among these discoveries is the growing number of confirmed extrasolar planets. New evidence also suggests that planets are the rule rather than the exception in star systems. For these reasons, increasing numbers of scientists have come to a momentous conclusion. Given enough time and the proper conditions, they say, some primitive organisms will invariably strive toward higher intelligence. "It certainly sounds," Shostak and Barnett

THE DRAKE EQUATION

In 1961, astronomer Frank Drake presented a mathematical equation that included all the relevant factors connected to the existence of possible alien civilizations. Each factor in the equation is estimated as a variable number or percentage.

$$R \times F_p \times n_e \times f_1 \times$$

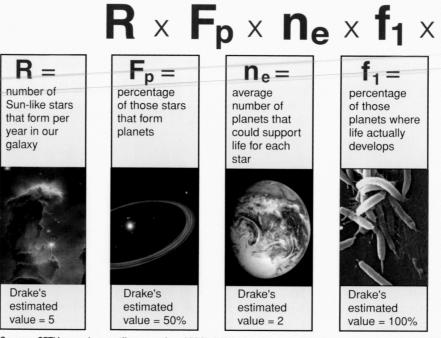

$R =$	$F_p =$	$n_e =$	$f_1 =$
number of Sun-like stars that form per year in our galaxy	percentage of those stars that form planets	average number of planets that could support life for each star	percentage of those planets where life actually develops
Drake's estimated value = 5	Drake's estimated value = 50%	Drake's estimated value = 2	Drake's estimated value = 100%

Sources: SETI League (www.setileague.org), and PBS's NOVA "Origins" series (http://www.pbs.org/wgbh/nova/origins).

write, "as if nature—whether on our planet or some alien world—will stumble into increased IQ sooner or later."[30]

CLASSIFYING INTELLIGENT ALIENS

Assuming that the optimists are right and at least a handful of sentient races have created civilizations in each galaxy, many people here on Earth would like to find some way to detect these races. But before this can be done with any degree of efficiency, such sentient aliens need to be categorized or classified in some way. After all, it is highly unlikely that they are all alike, either technologically or in other ways.

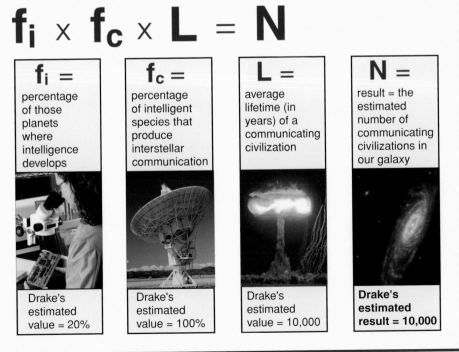

Scientists have evidence to make better guesses on some of the factors than on others. If one factor in the equation changes, the outcome will change accordingly. Since 1961, other scientists have used or modified this basic equation, which has since become known as the Drake equation.

$$f_i \times f_c \times L = N$$

f_i = percentage of those planets where intelligence develops

Drake's estimated value = 20%

f_c = percentage of intelligent species that produce interstellar communication

Drake's estimated value = 100%

L = average lifetime (in years) of a communicating civilization

Drake's estimated value = 10,000

N = result = the estimated number of communicating civilizations in our galaxy

Drake's estimated result = 10,000

Because galaxies like the Milky Way are many billions of years old, life is likely to appear and develop in random places and at random times in the history of a given galaxy. So some intelligent races may be very old, others very young, and many will have radically different levels of technology. As Seth Shostak puts it:

> It's extraordinarily unlikely that two random worlds, separated by hundreds or thousands of light-years, will develop in parallel. . . . The disparity will be such that there is little chance that aliens from two societies anywhere in the galaxy will be culturally close enough to really "get along." . . . This makes sense, given the overwhelmingly likely situation that galactic civilizations differ in their level of evolutionary development by thousands or millions of years.[31]

In this artist's conception, alien cities float in space. Such cities could make up part of the "surface" of a Dyson sphere.

©VICTOR HABBICK

Recognizing the need to categorize the intelligent alien civilizations that may exist, most scientists have adopted a system developed in 1964 by Russian physicist Nikolai Kardashev. He ranked such civilizations according to their ability to harness a given, measurable amount of energy. The more energy an alien race can tap into and manipulate, the more advanced it is on Kardashev's scale. That scale has three major levels. The first consists of Type I civilizations, each of which is capable of harnessing the entire potential energy output of a planet. At present, human society registers on the scale lower than a Type I (perhaps at the 0.7 level). This is because we still get most of our energy from burning coal and oil. Scientists who discuss the possibilities of advanced races of aliens consider such methods crude. Such scientists think that humanity may learn to make greater use of solar energy and nuclear fusion power and thereby become a Type I civilization within a century or two.

Next on Kardashev's scale come Type II civilizations, which have learned to tap the energy output of a single star such as the Sun. Not surprisingly, the Sun's output is enormous—up to 100 billion trillion horsepower at any given moment. A few years ago, American physicist Freeman Dyson suggested a way that a race of beings might manage to capture such huge quantities of radiant energy. They could, he said, build a gigantic sphere around their star. This "Dyson sphere," as it has come to be called, could be made up of billions of orbiting cities and energy-collecting satellites. Such a sphere might be invisible to Earth's searching eyes and telescopes. But its heat output would leak out into space in the form of infrared radiation, which humans might be able to detect.

The top level on Kardashev's scale is occupied by Type III civilizations. These are theoretically capable of utilizing the energy output of an entire galaxy. Such an advanced civilization would have so much energy at its disposal that it would have the potential to survive and thrive for a very long time, probably much longer than Type 1 and Type II civilizations. This realization led Carl Sagan and other researchers to conclude that at least one Type III civilization may presently exist in our own galaxy.

BEINGS BEYOND TECHNOLOGY?

Some scientists point out that Kardashev's system, though handy, may not be applicable to all alien races. His scale is based on technology. But what if some intelligent aliens do not possess technology in the conventional sense? Such beings may well have used traditional technology in their racial youth. But they may have somehow evolved beyond the need for technology or even ordinary physical forms.

Scientists have envisioned possible beings made up of highly organized energy fields floating in subzero space or unimaginably complex thermal currents swirling inside white-hot stars. American physicist Gerald Feinberg calls the hypothetical energy-field beings "radiobes" and the thermal beings "plasmobes."

It is probable that humans would not even recognize these beings as living things. But as weird as such life-forms may seem, some experts say that their possible existence cannot be dismissed. "While it's hard for modern-day scientists to imagine this form of life," Clifford Pickover points out, "remember that a century ago we could not contemplate the biochemistry of life on Earth."[32]

HOYLE'S EXOTIC CLOUD BEING

The classification of extraterrestrial civilizations according to their levels of technology presupposes that aliens will have and use technology. It also takes for granted that aliens will, like humans, have the sort of tangible, flesh-and-blood physical form with which we are familiar here on Earth. However, a number of scientists have pointed out that at least a few sentient ETs may have taken other, more exotic physical paths. One of the most striking suggestions for an exotic alien form came from the American astronomer Fred Hoyle. In his book *The Black Cloud*, he envisions an intelligent being thousands of miles long and composed of interstellar gases. These materials, he proposes, might be organized in a sophisticated manner by a complex, interactive energy field similar to the mass of firing neurons in the human brain. Such a cloud being would "feed" on the powerful energy fields generated by stars like the Sun. The cloud would reproduce by injecting sentient pieces of itself into a lifeless cloud of hydrogen gas, which would subsequently become increasingly organized and self-aware.

Astronomer Fred Hoyle believes an exotic alien cloud being could form from interstellar gases.

CHAPTER 5

Detecting Extraterrestrial Civilizations

The last four decades of the twentieth century witnessed a dramatic increase in the number of astronomers and other scientists who expressed confidence that sentient extraterrestrial life may exist. Their position has been well stated by one of the most famous of their number, the late Carl Sagan: "Once life has started in a relatively benign environment, and billions of years of evolutionary time are available," he said, "the expectation of many of us is that intelligent beings would develop."[33] This expectation is the driving force behind a series of ongoing searches for evidence of the existence of advanced alien races. These searches, collectively referred to as SETI (the Search for Extraterrestrial Intelligence), are designed to detect various kinds of signals given off by such races, either intentionally or unintentionally.

Though optimistic in some ways, SETI scientists are well aware that their chosen task is incredibly daunting. On the one hand, there are hundreds of billions of stars that must be examined in the Milky Way alone. Also, it is probable that only a small portion of any existing intelligent aliens will even be detectable.

Three leading SETI scientists, Peter Boyce, Jill Tarter, and Peter Backus, meet in 1995 to discuss ongoing SETI projects.

Remember that not all sentient races will be at the same technological level at any given time, including the present.

Ben Bova illustrates the problem with a colorful comparison. "Let our planet's 4.5 billion years be represented by the height of the Empire State Building," he says. "The thickness of a dime placed atop" the building "represents the entire span of our civilization—some 10,000 years." Then, he adds, place a postage stamp on the dime. The stamp represents the few hundred years that humanity has had advanced science. How many of the intelligent alien species in our galaxy "are within the thickness of that postage stamp?"[34] he asks. It will most likely be these civilizations—the ones with technology similar to our own—that will be detectable. This limitation imposed on SETI investigators has not discouraged them, however. They remain confident that, given enough time and patience, their efforts will be rewarded.

WHY LOOK BEYOND THE SOLAR SYSTEM?

Still, with only so much money, equipment, and manpower at their disposal, the SETI scientists recognize the need to allocate these resources carefully and wisely. This often means looking for alien life in places that seem remote and illogical to many nonscientists. For example, these researchers sometimes find themselves pressed to explain why their quest for intelligent life focuses only on distant stars. Many nonscientists think that sentient aliens exist and have probably visited our solar system. In fact, large segments of the public believe that alien spaceships have actually visited Earth. And many who hold this view think that scientists should first look for evidence of alien intelligence on Earth, the moon, or Mars.

Some advocates of this localized approach to SETI say that such evidence already exists. They cite numerous reports of sightings of so-called Unidentified Flying Objects, as well as claims that alien visitors have abducted humans and performed sinister experiments on them. Other believers point to photos taken by NASA probes that show what appears to be a large human-like face sculpted into a low hill on the surface of Mars. They argue that aliens constructed the face to get the attention of humans once the latter had developed space travel.

The "face" on Mars photographed in 1976 (left) and in 2001. The latter shows that the "eyes" and "mouth" were optical illusions.

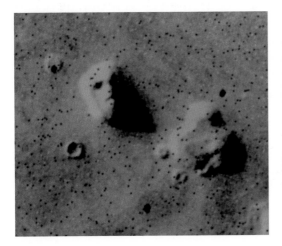

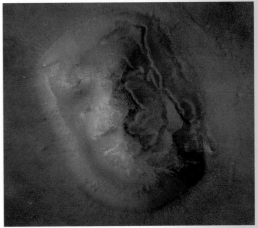

Scientists typically respond to such claims by pointing out that the burden of proof is on those who make them. So far, the consensus of scientists is that not a single piece of hard evidence has ever been presented that proves conclusively that aliens have visited Earth. (By hard evidence, they mean a sample of metal, wood, cloth, flesh, or some other material that can be examined in a lab and shown to be of extraterrestrial origin.) Regarding the so-called face on Mars, more recent photos of the hill in question indicate that the face's features are an optical illusion produced by sunlight hitting the hill at a particular angle.

This does not necessarily mean that no ETs have ever visited our solar system. Perhaps they did so in the past and left behind some sort of artifacts that would prove their existence. But as Shostak and Barnett point out, "The solar system is a big place and it's hard to comb it for . . . artifacts that might be no bigger than a car." Such searches would be "daunting and uncertain, and most researchers are unclear about how to start."[35] In short, SETI's limited resources would be better spent looking for something that everyone would immediately recognize as a sign of alien intelligence—an electronic or visual signal.

THE BIRTH OF SETI

Concerted, systematic searches for such signals began in the 1950s with the construction of large radio telescopes (antennas shaped like shallow bowls). Radio telescopes collect radio waves and other kinds of invisible radiation given off naturally by various cosmic objects. Two early advocates of radio astronomy—Italian astronomer Giuseppe Cocconi and American physicist Philip Morrison—realized that these big antennas might be used to detect artificial signals as well.

Cocconi and Morrison's reasoning went as follows. First, the great distances to other stars make sending mechanical probes to search for extraterrestrial life

USING RADIO TELESCOPES TO SEARCH FOR INTERSTELLAR SIGNALS

The main feature of a radio telescope is a large metallic dish that focuses radio waves and other kinds of invisible radiation onto the antenna. Most dishes are very large—from several feet to several hundred feet in diameter. The power of several radio telescopes can be combined to offer even more receptive power. These groups of radio telescopes are called arrays. Telescope arrays can consist of several telescopes placed next to one another, or in various locations spaced across the globe.

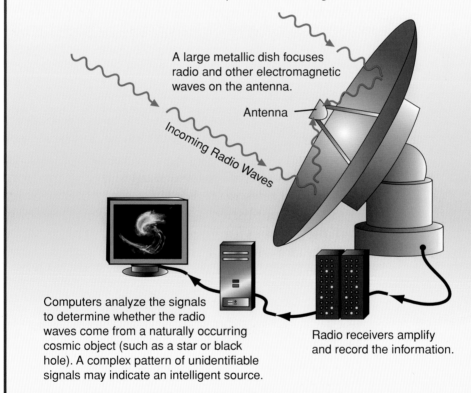

A large metallic dish focuses radio and other electromagnetic waves on the antenna.

Antenna

Incoming Radio Waves

Computers analyze the signals to determine whether the radio waves come from a naturally occurring cosmic object (such as a star or black hole). A complex pattern of unidentifiable signals may indicate an intelligent source.

Radio receivers amplify and record the information.

impractical. Even at 20 miles (32km) per second, the top speed of most NASA spacecraft, a probe would take forty thousand years just to reach the nearest star, Alpha Centauri. In contrast, radio waves, light rays, and other types of electromagnetic radiation travel at the speed of light—186,000 miles (299,274km) per second. So either receiving or sending electronic signals would be much faster and more practical.

This photo shows the huge dish of the Robert C. Byrd Green Bank Radio Telescope in Green Bank, West Virginia.

Also, Cocconi and Morrison realized, some radio waves readily penetrate interstellar gas and dust clouds, which hide the existence of many distant star systems from Earth's optical telescopes. For these and other reasons, in 1959 they published a scientific paper advocating systematic searches for intelligent aliens. "The presence of interstellar signals is entirely consistent with all we now know," they stated.

> And if signals are present, the means of detecting them is now at hand. Few will deny the profound importance, practical and philosophical, which the detection of interstellar communications would have. We therefore feel that a discriminating search for signals deserves a considerable effort. The probability of success is difficult to estimate, but if we never search, the chance of success is zero.[36]

Cocconi and Morrison's paper was one of the two major inspirations for the SETI programs that followed. The other was Project Ozma, launched by Frank Drake shortly before the paper was published.

(Drake named his search for intelligent ETs after Princess Ozma, a character in the Oz stories of L. Frank Baum.) Using the 85-foot-wide (26m) radio telescope at Green Bank, West Virginia, Drake investigated two nearby stars—Tau Ceti and Epsilon Eridani. He hoped to find some kind of artificial radio signal that could be shown to be from beyond Earth. No such signal was detected.

Nevertheless, Project Ozma, along with Cocconi and Morrison's paper, signaled to the scientific community that the time for a serious quest for ETs had come. "Suddenly the idea of searching for extraterrestrial intelligence became a hot topic," says Bova. Here were some "highly respected physicists saying it was not only possible to search, but desirable."[37] Accordingly, several other short-term SETI projects were launched in the United States, Canada, and Soviet Union.

THE COSMIC WATER HOLE

One of the difficulties that Drake and other early SETI pioneers faced was that millions of different frequencies of radio waves exist. Which of these would be most logical for an extraterrestrial race to use for sending signals into space? For one thing, scientists point out, any advanced ETs will know to avoid frequencies that are easily absorbed by interstellar gas clouds or planetary atmospheres, like Earth's. The reason is simple—signals sent at these frequencies will not make it very far or will be faint and unintelligible.

In contrast, some radio waves come through from their cosmic journeys loud and clear. Especially clear, and of particular interest to astronomers, are some frequencies in the low end of the microwave portion of the electromagnetic spectrum. First, there is the frequency of the natural radiation given off by hydrogen atoms floating in space—about 1,400 MHz (or 1.4 GHz). Close by is the frequency of the hydroxyl molecule, composed of one atom of hydrogen and one of oxygen—about 1,700 MHz (or 1.7 GHz).

When combined, an atom of hydrogen (H) and a hydroxyl molecule (OH) become a molecule of water (H_2O). For this reason, scientists called the region, or "window," between these two frequencies the cosmic "water hole." "The name is particularly apt," Isaac Asimov writes. First, water may well be one of the basic requirements of life throughout the universe. The water hole also conjures up a potent metaphor that all sentient beings might appreciate. "The hope is," Asimov continues, "that different civilizations will send and receive messages in this region as different species of animals come to drink at literal water holes on Earth."[38]

QUEST FOR THE "WOW!" SIGNAL

Using the water hole approach, among others, full-time searches for extraterrestrial signals began in the early 1980s with the foundation of the SETI Institute in Southern California. That facility employs more than 130 scientists, many of them Nobel Prize winners. Radio telescopes at observatories in the United States and other countries are also involved in the SETI effort. To date, these programs have studied a few thousand stars, most of them located in the Sun's general neighborhood, and no confirmed alien signals of any kind have been detected.

There *have* been a few tense and exciting moments when SETI scientists suspected they had received such signals. In 1977, for instance, an astronomer at an Ohio radio observatory detected a strong signal that seemed to be artificially designed. He was so excited that he wrote the word "Wow!" on the computer printout that recorded the radio source. But this unusual signal was never detected again by any radio telescope. Scientists agree that any genuine signal purposely sent by aliens will repeat many times to ensure that anyone who is listening receives it. Another incident occurred in 1997 at a West Virginia observatory. The researchers there detected a signal that was definitely of intelligent design.

But their moment of triumph was short-lived, as further investigation revealed that the signal was coming from a human-made satellite.

These and other false leads aside, does this cosmic silence indicate that sentient extraterrestrials do not exist? "Where is everybody?" Asimov asked. "Can it be that the development of intelligence on Earth is an unbelievably lucky chance, and that while the galaxy and universe swarm with life, even with land life, intelligence, and hence civilizations, might be altogether absent, except here?"[39] SETI scientists typically answer questions of this nature by reminding people that only a tiny fraction of stars in the Milky Way—less than one-thousandth of 1 percent—have been investigated so far. This is hardly a representative sampling, they say, and with the equipment presently available it could take centuries to examine them all.

Fortunately, results may come much sooner than that. This is because the number and, more importantly, the sophistication of radio telescopes are steadily improving. Presently under construction is the Allen Array, located a few hundred miles north of San Francisco.

AMATEUR SETI EFFORTS

The professional scientists engaged in the SETI searches have large radio telescopes and other sophisticated, expensive devices at their disposal. But that does not mean that interested amateurs cannot help in the quest to find alien signals. In fact, thousands of amateurs across the United States and in several foreign countries are presently doing just that. The most ambitious of the amateur SETI organizations is the SETI League, based in New Jersey. It has more than a hundred members who use small backyard satellite dishes to scan tiny selected regions of the sky, coordinating their efforts through the league. Like their professional counterparts, most of these amateurs tune their receivers to the frequencies of the water hole (1,400–1,700 MHz). Readers who would like to know more about the SETI League's activities or perhaps join the group can check out its Web site at www.setileague.org.

When completed in 2008, this facility will feature 350 separate radio dishes, each nearly 20 feet (6m) in diameter, spread over a tract of hundreds of acres. Scientists predict that this powerful instrument will allow them to examine up to a million stars in the first twenty years of operation alone. Other such advanced radio observatories are under construction in Canada, Australia, the Netherlands, and elsewhere.

OPTICAL SEARCHES FOR ETs

These sophisticated new radio antennas are not the only devices that scientists believe hold promise for detecting extraterrestrial signals. Some researchers have pointed out that sentient aliens who desire to communicate might also employ visual signals— more specifically, bright pulses of light produced by lasers. Indeed, it is the brightness of a tightly focused laser beam that makes it a potential tool for sending messages from one star system to another. Lasers existing right now on Earth can produce pulses of light some "5,000 times brighter than the Sun," Bova points out. Moreover, it does not matter how far away the observer is from the source.

> Both the [aliens' home] star's brightness and the brightness of the laser diminish at the same rate. A laser pulse that is 5,000 times brighter than the Sun will still be 5,000 times brighter than the Sun no matter how far away an observer may be. Thus, it should be easy to distinguish a deliberate laser pulse from the star near which it originates.[40]

The father, so to speak, of SETI's optical searches is English-born engineer Stuart A. Kingsley. In 1990, he inaugurated the Columbus Optical SETI Observatory in Columbus, Ohio. So far, his efforts to detect ETs, like those of radio observatories, have been unsuccessful. But Kingsley has inspired other researchers to launch optical searches, notably teams at the University of California at Berkeley and Harvard University in Massachusetts.

The SETI community is somewhat divided about the worth of the optical approach. Most scientists continue to believe that radio waves are a more promising medium than laser beams for sending interstellar messages. However, there is broad agreement among SETI researchers that optical searches are worth a try. "If we can do it, they can do it," Shostak and Barnett assert, comparing human and alien technologies. "So it seems to make eminently good sense to search for pulsing lights coming from the directions of neighborhood stars."[41]

These radio antennae are part of northern California's Allen Array, scheduled for completion in 2008.

Thus, if and when an alien signal is detected, it may come via radio waves or pulses of light. Or perhaps, to the surprise of human scientists, it will arrive in some other way. In the long run it will not matter, because it will be the message's very existence, not the medium, that will prove important for humanity. As one SETI researcher puts it:

> A SETI detection will tell us something that will forever change the way we view ourselves. Namely that we are only a single tile in a vast, cosmic mosaic. . . . The world will change overnight, and we will wake to find that all our histories, and all our stories are merely a small entry in an enormous book.[42]

SIGNALS FROM INTELLIGENT MACHINES?

Some scientists suggest that if humans do receive an alien signal, it may well have been sent by an intelligent machine rather than a flesh-and-blood being. In fact, the biological beings who built such a machine may have long ago died out, leaving their mechanical progeny to carry on their quest to communicate with other civilizations and acquire new knowledge. In *Cosmic Company*, SETI scientist Seth Shostak and his coauthor Alex Barnett speculate about this possibility:

> Extraterrestrials may have already constructed thinking machines. This would dramatically change the course of evolution on their planet, since cogitating computers can quickly improve themselves. . . . Clearly, once thinking machines are built, they can quickly overwhelm the abilities of biological intelligence. . . . So imagine the capabilities of thinking machines originally built by a galactic civilization that arrived at our technological level a billion years ago or more. . . . Unlike biological beings, machines (not being mortal) wouldn't balk at the idea of spending thousands of years rocketing between stars . . . in search of new knowledge.

CHAPTER 6

Opting to Communicate and Deciding What to Say

Many people today are excited about SETI because they are confident that sooner or later it will achieve success. One day in the near future, they fervently hope, an intelligent alien race will be detected and humans will be able to set up an interstellar dialogue with it. But some scientists are suspicious and a bit disturbed that purposeful signals of extraterrestrial origin have not already been detected. In their view, if the galaxy contains a number of intelligent races, even a small number, signals emitted by some of them should be coming through loud and clear right now. Why have we not detected any such signals, they ask?

Those researchers who are more optimistic about the existence of intelligent ETs have offered several logical answers to this question. For example, they say, one reason that no alien signals have been detected yet by the SETI programs may be that many extraterrestrial civilizations die out before they get around to sending out messages to the stars.

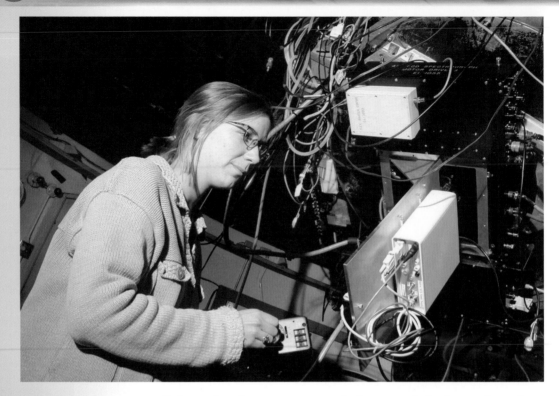

A physics student aligns a telescope at Lick Observatory to search for optical, or laser-like, signals from outer space.

It has also been suggested that, such beings, for what they view as compelling reasons, may have decided that they do not want to communicate with us—or with anyone else.

On a more optimistic note, some scientists say, one or more alien races may eagerly desire to communicate. And their messages may presently be on their way to Earth and may be detected at some future date. If so, the crucial question arises of how humans would respond to such a message. First, even if we determine that it is definitely of intelligent design, would we be able to decipher it? And if so, how should we answer it? What do humans consider most important about themselves and their planet to reveal to their cosmic cousins?

On the other hand, should humans reveal *anything* about themselves? A number of experts have pointed out the unpleasant possibility that some ETs may have sinister motives in sending out signals.

Perhaps they are trying to lure in unsuspecting intelligent races for the purpose of conquering or otherwise exploiting them.

All of these intriguing questions are routinely discussed and debated by SETI scientists and others interested in the existence of sentient alien life. They also consider what is perhaps the most momentous question of all: How will establishing contact with intelligent ETs affect and change human civilization?

THE FERMI PARADOX

One thing is certain. Sentient extraterrestrials will have no impact whatsoever on human civilization if said beings are not able or willing to communicate with us. The most extreme possibility in this regard is that no contact has been made with them and none will ever be made simply because they are not there. Some scientists have argued that if such beings did exist, they would already be here—that is, by now they would have arrived on Earth in spaceships and openly made contact.

The basic premise of this argument was stated in 1950 by the Nobel Prize–winning physicist Enrico Fermi. Where is everybody? he asked. What has come to be called the "Fermi paradox" in his honor goes as follows. Our galaxy is billions of years old, so there has been plenty of time for at least a few intelligent races to evolve. Ultimately, such races will develop space travel and push outward, establishing colonies and making contact in other star systems.

In 1950 physicist Enrico Fermi postulated the "Fermi paradox" to explain the impossibility of the existence of sentient extraterrestrials.

After millions or billions of years they should long ago have reached Earth, and since they obviously have not done so, they never existed in the first place.

Not surprisingly, SETI scientists reject this argument. Paraphrasing a famous remark by the great Carl Sagan, they frequently note that "absence of evidence is not equivalent to evidence of absence." In fact, a number of researchers point out that the Fermi paradox makes some assumptions that could be true but also could well not be true.

For example, the Fermi paradox assumes that all intelligent races survive long enough to develop advanced abilities in space travel. But it is entirely possible that many, or even most, extraterrestrial civilizations do not survive long enough to develop large-scale, far-reaching interstellar communication or exploration. Maybe they inevitably obliterate themselves with nuclear weapons or other destructive means. Isaac Asimov offers the following logical chain of reasoning:

> We can conclude that it is impossible for any species to be intelligent without coming to understand the meaning of competition, to foresee the dangers of losing out in competition . . . and to develop weapons of increasing power that will help them compete. Consequently, when the time comes where the weapons the intelligent species develops are so powerful and destructive that they outstrip the capacity of the species to recover and rebuild—the civilization automatically comes to an end. . . . Or civilization may just break down in internal violence. . . . We see this already [on Earth] in the rising tide of terrorism. Well, then, suppose that that is how it always is on any world. A civilization arrives, technological advance accelerates . . . and then civilization dies with a bang, or possibly with a whimper.[43]

COULD ALIENS SEND BLUEPRINTS OF THEMSELVES?

Some scientists have pointed out that some time in the foreseeable future it might be possible for humans to encode a digital message (using 1s and 0s, as in computer code) that describes the chemical breakdown of their own DNA. If this message was beamed to other worlds, any aliens who received and decoded it would know the exact makeup of the human body. Following this blueprint, they might even be able to combine the appropriate chemicals and other materials in their labs and construct a human being (assuming they possess technology that is sufficiently sophisticated). Conversely, at some future time humans might be able to reconstruct an alien from genetic instructions sent in an electronic message, an idea first suggested by the noted American astronomer Fred Hoyle in the 1960s. It should be emphasized, however, that any human or alien created this way would be a blank slate, mentally speaking, as knowledge, memories, and personality could not be programmed and included in the message.

Another possibility is that some or many interstellar civilizations are wiped out by large-scale cosmic disasters. Indeed, big impacts by asteroids and comets have occurred several times on Earth, causing mass extinctions. It is certain that planets everywhere suffer such large impact events from time to time, and it is probable that at least some intelligent races have been destroyed this way. Supernovas—the titanic explosions of unstable stars observed periodically by astronomers—constitute another cosmic threat to planets and the life inhabiting them. Also, even if such a catastrophe does not destroy all intelligent beings on a planet, the survivors may never again be able to regain their former level of prosperity and technology.

CAN OR SHOULD CONTACT BE MADE?

Scientists have pointed out other reasons why intelligent ETs might not be able, or perhaps might not want, to reveal their presence, all of which constitute perfectly believable exceptions to the Fermi paradox.

Some extraterrestrial civilizations may be warlike and bent on conquest, as depicted in popular movies such as Independence Day.

One possibility is that the enormous distances that separate stars and galaxies may make interstellar communication and travel too arduous and costly an undertaking for large numbers of alien races. "The vast majority of civilizations, conceivably all of them, may simply remain in their own planetary systems," Asimov suggests, and not even bother to attempt to make contact with other civilizations.

> Any interstellar probes that are sent out [by such aliens] may be devices not designed to land on habitable planets but to confine themselves to observations and reports from space. . . . In this way, we can rationalize the apparent paradox that while the galaxy may be rich in civilizations, we remain unaware of them.[44]

Another possible reason that no alien races have made contact or sent spaceships to Earth may be a simple accident in timing. What if humanity is among the first, or even *the* first, intelligent race in our galaxy to create a technological civilization? If so, other civilizations may not have had time to develop either the means of interstellar travel or the devices needed to send messages to the stars.

Another objection to the Fermi paradox involves the cultural, political, and/or religious concepts and values of the ETs. Even if some of them do possess advanced technology, perhaps they have legal, religious, or other taboos about using it in the ways we do. It is also possible that they simply have no interest whatsoever in space. The Fermi paradox presupposes that all intelligent beings everywhere will have the same mental outlook, values, desires, and racial goals, but there is no reason why this should be the case.

Some scientists have offered still another reason why contact, either by signals or in person, has not been made with alien races. It is possible, they say, that intelligent beings do know about humanity's existence but have placed Earth under a sort of quarantine. On the one hand, the ETs may view humans as somehow odd, inferior, or dangerous and have made Earth off-limits. On the other hand, the aliens may believe it is unethical to interfere in the internal affairs of other cultures until those cultures reach a certain level of development. This is the basis for the famous "prime directive" in the *Star Trek* universe: Federation vessels are allowed to observe developing civilizations from a discreet distance, but they must not reveal their presence until the natives develop the means of traveling beyond their home star systems.

Finally, there is the possibility that intelligent aliens have not made contact because they have bad intentions. They may be maintaining radio silence, listening and patiently searching for other civilizations to exploit. If this is the case, humanity's attempt to establish contact with alien intelligence may be a huge and fatal mistake. "Suppose there *are* civilizations out there as vicious and warlike as we ourselves are at our worst . . . who *are* looking for prey, and who have until now been unaware of us?" Asimov asks. "Shouldn't we lie low and be absolutely quiet?"[45]

Asimov and other scientists have answered this question by advocating that SETI redouble its efforts. Thus far, these efforts have been for listening for alien signals, not sending signals to the stars. According to this view, the more we can learn about alien motives by listening, the better informed we can be about how safe it is to attempt contact.

COMPOSING COSMIC MESSAGES

So far, the discussion has focused mainly on the negative possibilities of contact with intelligent aliens. On the positive side, in contrast, it could well be that few or no aliens have bad motives. And perhaps a number of galactic civilizations manage not to annihilate themselves. Moreover, maybe a good many of them do wish to establish contact with other sentient races.

Assuming these optimistic probabilities are true, what kind of messages should humans send to intelligent ETs? First, humans need to decide on a medium or "language" that is likely to be understood by any and all intelligent beings. Also, we need to decide what specific information about humanity is essential to convey in the early stages of an interstellar dialogue.

Intelligent beings on other worlds will have their own languages, which will undoubtedly differ greatly from any human tongue. But all scientists agree that there is a sort of universal language that sentient creatures everywhere will readily recognize—mathematics. The symbols that aliens use for 1, 2, 3, +, −, and X will be different, of course, but the basic concepts will be the same, or else they could not have developed advanced technology.

One of the first questions that early SETI scientists asked was how humans might convey these basic mathematical concepts to any aliens that might be listening. Frank Drake promptly answered this question by developing a simplified prototype in 1961. It consisted of a message made up of 551 1s and 0s arranged in a sequence similar to the binary digital code used in computers. Drake showed that, when arranged in a certain order and correctly deciphered, these few numbers could be used to convey surprisingly large amounts of information. Scientists are confident that digital messages of this sort will be a workable medium to employ if and when they decide to begin systematic attempts to make cosmic contact. (So far, only one such message has been sent, partly as a test and partly as a lark. In 1974, the Arecibo Radio Telescope, in Puerto Rico, sent a brief digital message similar to Drake's toward a star cluster some twenty-one thousand light-years away. Obviously, any response will take forty-two thousand years to get here.)

Some idea of the content of cosmic messages humans may send comes from the one etched into a plaque carried by NASA's *Pioneer 10*. Launched in 1972, the probe flew by and photographed the planet Jupiter, then moved out of the solar system and into

EARLY PLANS FOR SENDING COSMIC MESSAGES

The universality of mathematics and its potential use to contact intelligent ETs was understood as far back as the nineteenth century. In the early 1800s, a German mathematician, Karl F. Gauss, proposed signaling the possible inhabitants of Mars by creating a huge right triangle on Earth's surface. Lanes of different colored crops would be planted, making big squares along each of the triangle's sides. This would demonstrate to the Martians that humans understand the Pythagorean theorem. One of Gauss's contemporaries, Austrian astronomer Joseph J. von Littrow, suggested that people dig long ditches arranged in mathematical patterns. They could then pour kerosene into the ditches and set them on fire at night, hopefully attracting the attention of beings on other worlds. Obviously such crude means would only be useful if the beings dwelled on planets very near Earth. And science has shown that no advanced ETs live in our solar system. However, a more sophisticated mathematical approach could be used for contacting aliens inhabiting other star systems.

interstellar space. Carl Sagan and Frank Drake attached the aluminum plaque, measuring 6 by 9 inches (15 by 23cm), in hopes that some future alien space-farers might find it. In a sequence of 1s and 0s, the message first identifies the hydrogen atom, the most basic building block of the universe. The message also provides the location of Earth, the probe's home planet, and shows the other planets in the Sun's family. A diagram shows a man and a woman standing in front of a schematic of the probe; that way, anyone who finds it will see what humans look like and know how big they are. These details are similar to ones in Drake's 1961 digital message, which noted that human body chemistry is based on carbon and

In 1972 American astronomer Carl Sagan holds the plaque he and Frank Drake designed for the Pioneer 10 *probe.*

that humans are oxygen breathers. These are the same kinds of basic facts that SETI scientists expect to find in alien messages beamed to Earth.

A PROFOUND IMPACT

If and when such messages from the stars arrive and are deciphered, SETI researchers point out, the impact on human society will be profound. The human race's view of the universe and of itself will be fundamentally and permanently altered. First, the aliens making contact may be willing to share part or all of their accumulated knowledge with us. If they are thousands or millions of years ahead of humanity in science, they will have developed the means of producing abundant energy. And acquiring this and other advanced technology would allow humans to eliminate poverty, hunger, disease, and other large-scale problems almost overnight.

The establishment of contact with intelligent ETs will almost surely impact Earth's religions as well. The aliens may have completely different religious concepts and values, or perhaps none at all. These beings may believe that they have discovered the true meaning of spirituality or that they are closer to God than members of less advanced civilizations. If so, they may dismiss human religious ideas and urge people to think and worship as they do. Any of these scenarios could significantly influence or alter the religious ideas and practices of many of Earth's inhabitants.

At least these are some of the things that scientists and other experts predict are likely to happen as a result of first contact with sentient ETs. It is possible, of course, that some or all of them may *not* happen. As Alan Rubin puts it: "It is hard to predict the ultimate consequences of the detection of alien messages. The only sure bet is that we would finally know that we are not alone and that other societies have survived their technological adolescence."[46]

CHAPTER 7

Inventing Ways to Meet Face-to-Face

If humans ever do detect the presence of an extraterrestrial civilization, there is little doubt that they will acknowledge receipt of the alien message by sending out one of their own. After all, the benefits that humanity might reap from setting up an interstellar dialogue might be great. But it is important to understand that the difficulties of establishing and maintaining such cosmic communications are immense. This is partly because the distances between stars are enormous. The messages sent and received travel at the speed of light, which is very fast by human standards but very slow by cosmic ones. If the aliens who have been detected inhabit a planet lying ten thousand light-years away, our message will take ten thousand years to reach them. And their answer will take another ten thousand years to reach us. Even if the ETs in question live only fifty light-years away, each exchange of messages will take a century.

Under these conditions, therefore, even the simplest interstellar dialogue will be extremely time-consuming and frustrating. And it is doubtful that humans will be patient enough just to sit back and wait for each new message to arrive. A majority of scientists are convinced that humanity, and many alien races as well, will prefer to take the final step in the communication process—a face-to-face meeting. Indeed, some researchers say, the receipt of an alien message, on whatever planet it is received, may become a sort of call to arms for launching interstellar probes. Some of these might be robots with no one aboard. But ultimately such vehicles will have pilots and passengers who are eager to shake hands (or claws, or tentacles?) with their cosmic cousins.

These stars lie more than 5,000 light-years away. A signal from one of them would take that long to reach Earth.

One major obstacle stands in the way of this dream of establishing physical contact with ETs, however. It is the same one that makes exchanging interstellar messages so difficult, namely the great distances from one star system to another. Indeed, says astronomer John W. Macvey:

> The overriding factor is distance—distance of such magnitude that the supposed "high" velocities that have taken men to the moon and instrumented probes to . . . Jupiter would be quite useless with respect to a journey even to the *nearest* star unless our lifetimes were of the order of many thousands of years.[47]

Does that mean that such journeys to the stars are impossible? Not necessarily, a number of scientists say. In fact, the consensus of most physicists and planetary scientists is that, given sufficiently advanced technology, there may well be ways to get around the interstellar distance problem. Moreover, considering the age of the universe and our galaxy, it does seem possible, if not probable, that someone

The fictional starship Enterprise *uses "warp drive" to travel faster than light. In reality, however, such speeds are likely impossible.*

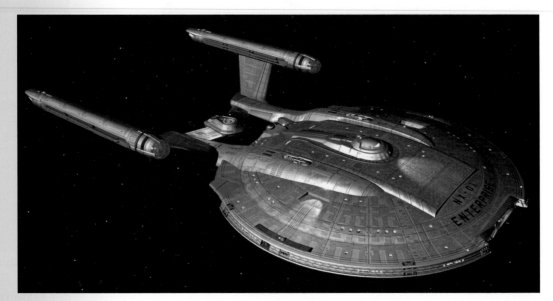

has already acquired such advanced technology. "Our galaxy is some 10 billion years old," Macvey points out, "and contains something on the order of 100 billion stars. It is hard to believe that in all this myriad host of suns and throughout all these countless millennia not one race has developed without achieving a degree of practical interstellar capability."[48] What are the chances that this has happened? And how might humans develop such capabilities and use them to establish face-to-face contact with distant sentient races?

PROBLEMS WITH SUPER LIGHT SPEED

One often suggested approach to overcoming the problem of vast interstellar distances is to discover some way of making spacecraft move faster. In fact, this is the most common solution to the problem as depicted in the *Star Trek* universe and other fictional realms. The starship *Enterprise* and other futuristic space vessels use "warp drive," "hyperdrive," or other advanced propulsion systems that allow them to hurtle through space at speeds surpassing the speed of light.

If only it were that easy, say physicists and astronomers. The reality is that, as the great German American physicist Albert Einstein pointed out in the early 1900s, nothing can surpass the speed of light. "Physics becomes full of impossibilities if super light speed is allowed," physicist Lawrence M. Krauss explains.

> Not least among the problems is that because objects get more massive as they approach the speed of light, it takes progressively more and more energy to accelerate them by a smaller and smaller amount. . . . All the energy in the universe would not be sufficient to allow us to push even a speck of dust, much less a starship, past this ultimate speed limit.[49]

Another dilemma is that even if humans *could* achieve super light speeds, they would be confronted with some bizarre alterations in the flow and duration of time. While their vessel was traveling faster than light, time would seem to pass quite normally. In the world outside the ship, however, hundreds, thousands, or even millions of years would be elapsing. When the crew of the ship returned to Earth, therefore, everyone they had known would be long dead. In fact, they might even find that humanity had become extinct while they were away. Thus, Krauss points out, "a 10-year journey for the *Enterprise* would correspond to a 25,000-year period for Starfleet Command," and this "would wreak havoc on any command operation that hoped to organize and control the movements of many such craft."[50]

Is Hibernation Practical?

Numerous scientists and writers have been undaunted by this seemingly impenetrable ceiling nature has placed on speed. In the past century, and especially in the past few decades, they have proposed several possible alternatives to super light speeds. Most of these methods assume that the journey will be very long and seek ways to make the passage of so much time bearable for the travelers.

For instance, one way that either humans or aliens might make practical interstellar trips is by hibernating, or achieving what is often called a state of "suspended animation." The crew of a ship would go to sleep shortly after leaving its home star system and wake up just before or after the vessel entered the target system. During such a journey, onboard computers and other advanced devices would run the ship, keep it on course, and repair it if it was damaged. These machines would also carefully monitor the life signs and health of the sleeping crew.

At first glance, this approach to interstellar travel sounds doable and practical, given that the beings

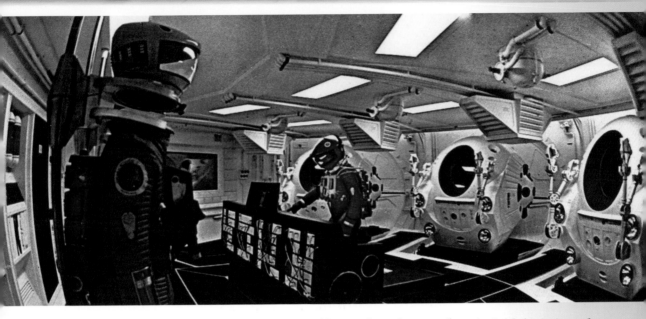

who undertake the project have sufficiently advanced technology. Like super light travel, however, hibernation has some serious limitations. First, putting the crew of a spacecraft to sleep will be practical only for trips to the nearest stars. Even if the vessel can travel 1,000 miles (1,609km) per second—more than fifty times the speed of NASA's *Voyager* and *Galileo* craft— a journey to a star a thousand light-years away (only 1/100 the width of the Milky Way) will take some 200,000 years. No matter how advanced human or alien technology becomes, it may well be that sleeping that long is neither possible nor desirable.

Some scientists have tried to get around this problem by suggesting that at least some alien species may have developed life spans many times longer than human ones. This is certainly possible. But it, too, has limits when applied to interstellar journeys. Even if a hypothetical ET could live as long as 10,000 years, and this was extended to 100,000 years through the hibernation process, it would not survive the 200,000-year hibernation period described above. Moreover, any trips the ET makes to fairly nearby star systems would still consume much of its life.

A vivid depiction of the use of hibernation for space travelers appeared in Stanley Kubrick's 1968 film 2001: A Space Odyssey.

It is highly doubtful that said space traveler would ever see its home planet again. And it is difficult to imagine anyone, whether human or alien, who would willingly sleep away most or all of its life in the lonely depths of space.

GENERATION SHIPS

But what if human or alien space travelers could be awake all through an interstellar trip? This is a basic premise of the concept of the generation ship, which some scientists have called a "space ark." It would consist of a huge spaceship—more properly a flying space city or colony—in which dozens, hundreds, or even thousands of generations of travelers would live and die on the voyage. In the case of such an expedition, all those involved would understand from the start that they would never be returning to Earth. Rather, their great-great-great- (and likely many more greats!) grandchildren would be the ones privileged to have the first face-to-face encounters with extraterrestrials.

Some engineers and other scientists have already created preliminary designs for generation ships. These have incorporated certain fundamental features required to support hundreds or thousands of people for centuries or perhaps millennia. First, such a vessel would need to be a self-contained world big enough to support tracts of farmland, so that the inhabitants could grow most of their food. In fact, "such space settlements would not carry supplies of food and oxygen in the ordinary sense," according to Isaac Asimov. "They would be in a functioning ecological balance that could maintain itself indefinitely, given a secure energy source,"[51] such as nuclear fusion (a controlled version of the process that makes the stars shine). Therefore, the inhabitants would also need large water supplies in the form of lakes and streams, as well as houses and towns to live in.

The shapes of the generation ships that have already been designed differ somewhat. But most are variations of the cylinder, or soup can, shape. The inhabitants would live and work on the cylinder's curved inside surface, and they and their houses and belongings would stay on the "ground" thanks to artificial gravity created by spinning the ship.

Some scientists and writers have pointed out possible drawbacks of such vessels. First, they would be enormously expensive and difficult to build. And considering that a generation ship and its crew would never return to Earth, many investors might feel there is not enough of an incentive or potential payoff to justify such huge expenditures of money, resources, and time.

This is one of several designs for a generation ship, which would have onboard greenhouses and farms.

THE ANT AND THE WATERMELON

Some scientists think that manipulating a wormhole in just the right way might allow a spaceship to travel to distant star systems in a fraction of the time it would take if the vessel was moving through ordinary space. These researchers frequently employ the analogy of an ant and a watermelon. The outer surface of the melon represents normal space. The ant, which is walking on the melon, represents a spacecraft on a long journey to a distant location on the opposite side of the melon. Even when moving as fast as it can, the ant requires three full minutes to complete the trip. Just before setting out, however, the creature sees a nearby hole, the mouth of a tunnel that appears to go straight into the heart of the melon. The ant thinks twice about entering the hole because it seems to lead into an unknown region very different from the familiar realm of the surface. But the ant finally decides to take a chance and crawls down the hole. Following the tunnel, the ant travels straight through the center of the melon and climbs out of another hole on the opposite side, right beside its destination. The creature is happy to discover that the route it chose is shorter and more direct than the one on the surface, so the trip took only one minute instead of three.

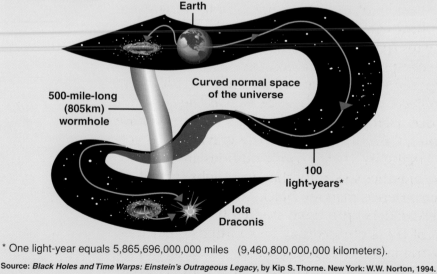

Some scientists think that traveling through a wormhole might allow a spaceship to travel to a distant star system in much less time than it would take to travel through ordinary space. Since the universe is not contained on one flat plane, it is possible that a wormhole could offer such a shortcut.

Earth

500-mile-long
(805km)
wormhole

Curved normal space
of the universe

100
light-years*

Iota
Draconis

* One light-year equals 5,865,696,000,000 miles (9,460,800,000,000 kilometers).

Source: *Black Holes and Time Warps: Einstein's Outrageous Legacy*, by Kip S. Thorne. New York: W.W. Norton, 1994.

Also, some experts warn, too many things could go wrong on such a long mission into the unknown and untamed depths of space. The vessel might be crippled or destroyed by a collision with an asteroid, for example, or a disease epidemic of mysterious origins could wipe out the crew. In later generations political disputes could lead to a civil war resulting in the ship's destruction. Or the war could kill most of the inhabitants and reduce the survivors to savages whose descendants no longer know where they came from and where they are going. Still another plausible scenario envisions a later generation of the travelers deciding to abandon the mission and begin colonizing uninhabited planets they have encountered in their journey.

WORMHOLES AND CHILDHOOD'S END

In fact, some scientists think that so many things could go wrong on a generation ship on a long voyage that all such journeys are doomed to end in failure. And this might well be why no such ships have ever visited our solar system (at least in human memory). But if faster-than-light travel, hibernation, and generation ships are all ultimately impractical for long space voyages, how can humans and aliens hope to bridge the vast gaps that separate them and meet in person?

Some scientists say that a possible answer may lie in the purposeful manipulation of some of the most bizarre objects in the universe, as well as the very fabric of space itself. The strange objects in question are black holes. Often the result of the gravitational collapse of large stars, these cosmic oddities are so dense and have gravities so strong that even light cannot escape them. Hence they are black. According to many of the researchers who have studied black holes, the gravities of these objects may be so intense that they can tear the fabric of space, creating small openings. Such openings and the invisible spatial tunnels scientists believe they lead to are together commonly called wormholes.

Depictions of wormholes and piloted spacecraft traveling through them have become common-place in modern science fiction books, movies, and television shows. But however fantastic they may seem in such stories, wormholes cannot be written off as purely fictional. In the past century, several physicists have used mathematics to show that these cosmic gateways are theoretically possible. In 1935, for instance, Einstein and a colleague, Nathan Rosen, examined the concept of a sort of tunnel that might exist inside a black hole. For a while, researchers called such cosmic tunnels "Einstein-Rosen bridges," after the men who first proposed them. Only later did they acquire the name wormholes. In the 1980s, another brilliant physicist—Kip Thorne, of the California Institute of Technology—updated and expanded on Einstein and Rosen's calculations. Thorne showed how a wormhole might allow matter to enter hyperspace, a region lying beyond normal space, and exit back into space at another similar portal.

Since that time, other scientists have cautioned that, although wormholes may exist, it may not be safe for flesh-and-blood beings to travel through them. First, the gravitational effects of the black hole surrounding the wormhole would almost surely crush an approaching person or spaceship. Even if some kind of special shielding could be made to prevent this danger, the wormhole's walls might collapse, killing the traveler.

Of course, it is possible that advanced technologies far beyond anything we can imagine now have made it possible for aliens to travel through wormholes safely. If so, these gateways may provide short-cuts such beings use to reach distant worlds. Perhaps journeys that would normally take thousands or millions of years are (or will someday be) possible in only days, hours, or even minutes! In that case, Carl Sagan points out,

The deaths of massive stars [a process that often creates black holes, which in turn spawn wormholes] may provide the means for transcending the present boundaries of space and time, making all the universe accessible to life—and in the last deep sense—unifying the cosmos.[52]

Someday, therefore—perhaps soon, or maybe centuries from now—living beings that sprang from different chemistries in oceans separated by many light-years may meet and share their knowledge and experiences. If it happens, it will be the greatest event in history and the end of humanity's cosmic childhood.

A spacecraft exits a wormhole in this artist's conception. Some scientists believe that such cosmic tunnels actually exist.

NOTES

INTRODUCTION: THE BEGINNING OF TRUE UNDERSTANDING?

1. Quoted in Ben Bova, *Faint Echoes, Distant Stars: The Science and Politics of Finding Life Beyond Earth*. New York: William Morrow, 2004, p. ix.

2. Quoted in *Life of Epicurus*, in Diogenes Laertius, *Lives of Eminent Philosophers*, trans. R.D. Hicks. 2 vols. Cambridge, MA: Harvard University Press, 1995, 2:575.

3. Quoted in Clifford Pickover, *The Science of Aliens*. New York: Basic, 1999, p. 13.

4. Steven J. Dick, *Life on Other Worlds*. New York: Cambridge University Press, 1998, pp. 8–9.

5. David Koerner and Simon LeVay, *Here Be Dragons: The Scientific Quest for Extraterrestrial Life*. New York: Oxford University Press, 2000, pp. 237–38.

6. Bova, *Faint Echoes, Distant Stars*, p. 284.

CHAPTER 1: HUNTING FOR EARTH-LIKE PLANETS

7. Bova, *Faint Echoes, Distant Stars*, p. 214.

8. Tim Appenzeller, "Search for Other Earths," *National Geographic*, December 2004, p. 79.

9. Seth Shostak and Alex Barnett, *Cosmic Company: The Search for Life in the Universe*. New York: Cambridge University Press, 2003, pp. 32–33.

10. Appenzeller, "Search for Other Earths," p. 95.

CHAPTER 2: EXPLORING THE SUN'S WATER WORLDS

11. Shostak and Barnett, *Cosmic Company*, p. 15.

12. Alan Longstaff, "Quest for a Living Universe," *Astronomy*, April 2005, p. 33.

13. Richard Talcott, "An Ice Moon Revealed," *Astronomy*, July 2005, pp. 64–65.

14. Robert Pappalardo, "Jupiter's Water Worlds," *Astronomy*, July 2004, pp. 38, 40.

15. Gerald A. Soffen, *Life in the Solar System,"* in J. Kelly Beatty et al., *The New Solar System.* Cambridge, UK: Cambridge University Press, 1999, p. 369.

16. Pappalardo, *Jupiter's Water Worlds,"* p. 37.

17. Pappalardo, *Jupiter's Water Worlds,"* p. 41.

CHAPTER 3: SEEKING THE BUILDING BLOCKS OF LIFE

18. Bova, *Faint Echoes, Distant Stars*, p. 28.

19. Alan E. Rubin, *Disturbing the Solar System: Impacts, Close Encounters, and Coming Attractions.* Princeton, NJ: Princeton University Press, 2002, p. 289.

20. Bova, *Faint Echoes, Distant Stars*, pp. 179–80.

21. Bova, *Faint Echoes, Distant Stars*, p. 148.

22. Isaac Asimov, *Extraterrestrial Civilizations.* New York: Fawcett, 1988, pp. 160–61.

23. Paul Davies, *Are We Alone? Philosophical Implications of the Discovery of Extraterrestrial Life.* New York: Basic, 1996, p. 13.

24. Pickover, *Science of Aliens*, pp. 108–09.

25. Soffen, "Life in the Solar System," p. 369.

CHAPTER 4: WEIGHING THE CHANCES OF ALIEN INTELLIGENCE

26. Alfred Russel Wallace, *Man's Place in the Universe.* London: Chapman and Hall, 1904, p. 335.

27. Quoted in Dick, *Life on Other Worlds*, p. 195.

28. Terence Dickinson and Adolf Schaller, *Extraterrestrials: A Field Guide for Earthlings.* Topeka, KS: Rebound by Sagebrush, 2001, p. 28.

29. Shostak and Barnett, *Cosmic Company*, p. 64.

30. Shostak and Barnett, *Cosmic Company*, p. 67.

31. Seth Shostak, *Sharing the Universe: Perspectives on Extraterrestrial Life*. Berkeley, CA: Berkeley Hills, 1998, p. 96.

32. Pickover, *Science of Aliens*, p. 101.

CHAPTER 5: DETECTING EXTRATERRESTRIAL CIVILIZATIONS

33. Carl Sagan, *The Dragons of Eden*. New York: Ballantine, 1977, p. 240.

34. Bova, *Faint Echoes, Distant Stars*, p. 251.

35. Shostak and Barnett, *Cosmic Company*, pp. 95–96.

36. Quoted in Bova, *Faint Echoes, Distant Stars*, p. 21.

37. Bova, *Faint Echoes, Distant Stars*, p. 234.

38. Asimov, *Extraterrestrial Civilizations*, p. 267.

39. Asimov, *Extraterrestrial Civilizations*, pp. 178, 186.

40. Bova, *Faint Echoes, Distant Stars*, p. 253.

41. Shostak and Barnett, *Cosmic Company*, p. 111.

42. Shostak and Barnett, *Cosmic Company*, p. 156.

CHAPTER 6: OPTING TO COMMUNICATE AND DECIDING WHAT TO SAY

43. Asimov, *Extraterrestrial Civilizations*, pp. 192–93.

44. Asimov, *Extraterrestrial Civilizations*, p. 249.

45. Asimov, *Extraterrestrial Civilizations*, p. 255.

46. Rubin, *Disturbing the Solar System*, p. 320.

CHAPTER 7: INVENTING WAYS TO MEET FACE-TO-FACE

47. John W. Macvey, *Interstellar Travel: Past, Present, and Future*. Bath, UK: Scarborough House, 1991, p. 10.

48. Macvey, *Interstellar Travel*, p. 20.

49. Lawrence M. Krauss, *The Physics of* Star Trek. New York: HarperCollins, 1995, p. 23.

50. Krauss, *The Physics of* Star Trek, pp. 22–23.

51. Asimov, *Extraterrestrial Civilizations*, p. 242.

52. Carl Sagan, *The Cosmic Connection: An Extraterrestrial Perspective*. New York: Dell, 1973, p. 267.

GLOSSARY

amino acids: Organic compounds found in proteins, the building blocks of living tissue.

ammonia: A colorless, poisonous gas made up of the elements nitrogen and hydrogen.

aquatic: Water-based; living in the ocean.

asteroid: A small stony or metallic body orbiting the Sun, most often in the asteroid belt lying between the planets Mars and Jupiter.

black hole: A superdense object with gravity so strong that not even light can escape it.

Dyson sphere: A huge shell constructed around a star with the purpose of capturing and exploiting the star's energy.

electromagnetic spectrum: The range of different kinds of visible and invisible radiation, including visual light, ultraviolet light, X-rays, radio waves, and others.

extrasolar: Existing beyond the solar system.

extraterrestrial (ET): A living thing originating beyond Earth; relating to such a being.

extremophiles: Living things that exist and thrive in environments that are harsh, poisonous, or otherwise extreme for humans and most other Earth creatures.

galaxy: A gigantic group of stars held together by their combined gravities. Our galaxy is called the Milky Way.

habitable zone: The region in a star system in which liquid water can exist on planetary surfaces, providing a friendly environment for the development of life.

hyperspace: A hypothetical region lying outside of and invisible from ordinary space.

interstellar: Between stars, usually referring to travel from one star to another.

light-year: The distance that light travels in a year, or about 6 trillion miles (9.654 trillion km).

NASA: The National Aeronautics and Space Administration, the U.S. government agency in charge of learning about and exploring the universe.

orbit: To move around something; the path taken by a planet, comet, or asteroid around the sun, or by a moon around a planet.

organic materials: Substances making up the building blocks of living things.

organism: A plant, animal, or other living thing.

radio telescope: A large, bowl-shaped antenna designed to collect radio waves and other kinds of electromagnetic radiation.

sentient: Having enough intelligence to be conscious, self-aware, and capable of creating a technical civilization.

SETI: The Search for Extraterrestrial Intelligence; a collection of programs organized to seek out signals from alien civilizations.

solar system: The Sun and all the objects that orbit it.

stellar: Having to do with stars.

supernova: A tremendous explosion that occurs during the gravitational collapse of a large star. The gases and other debris sent flying by the explosion are called the supernova remnant.

thermal: Having to do with heat.

Type I civilization: A civilization with the capability of harnessing the energy output of a planet.

Type II civilization: A civilization with the capability of harnessing the energy output of a star.

Type III civilization: A civilization with the capability of harnessing the energy output of a galaxy.

universe: The total of all the space and matter known to exist.

wormhole: A theoretical invisible tunnel connecting a black hole to another spot in the universe.

FOR FURTHER READING

BOOKS

Jack Cohen and Ian Stewart, *What Does a Martian Look Like? The Science of Extraterrestrial Life*. New York: Wiley, 2002. A well- and simply written introduction to the subject.

Terence Dickinson and Adolf Schaller, *Extraterrestrials: A Field Guide for Earthlings*. Topeka, KS: Rebound by Sagebrush, 2001. Easy to read and beautifully illustrated, this is a good starting point for those who are unfamiliar with the subject.

Simon Goodwin and John Gribbon, *XTL: Extraterrestrial Life and How to Find It*. London: Weidenfeld and Nicolson, 2003. Two scientists present the basics of current arguments for the existence of ET life.

Nigel Henbest, *DK Space Encyclopedia*. London: Dorling Kindersley, 2000. This beautifully mounted and critically acclaimed book is the best general source available for grade school readers about the wonders of space.

WEB SITES

Astrobiology.Com (www.astrobiology.com). Lists numerous links leading to useful information about current research and projects relating to space travel and ET life.

NASA Astrobiology Institute (http://nai.arc.nasa.gov). An online venue partly supported by NASA for the promotion of interest and research in the area of life beyond Earth.

Planetary Society (www.planetary.org). Home page of the Planetary Society, a leading advocacy group that promotes research into space travel and related subjects.

SETI Institute (www.seti.org). Home page of the SETI Institute, providing the latest ongoing information about the exciting search for ET life.

WORKS CONSULTED

MAJOR WORKS

Isaac Asimov, *Extraterrestrial Civilizations*. New York: Fawcett, 1988. Slightly dated, but still one of the two or three best general discussions of the subject, including a great deal of technical information presented in an easy-to-read manner.

John Billingham et al., eds., *Social Implications of Detection of an Extraterrestrial Intelligenc*e. Mountain View, CA: SETI, 1999. A collection of essays by experts, each covering one or more ways that human society may react to the discovery of alien beings.

Ben Bova, *Faint Echoes, Distant Stars: The Science and Politics of Finding Life Beyond Earth*. New York: William Morrow, 2004. An extremely thoughtful synopsis of human efforts to determine if life may exist beyond Earth. Highly recommended.

Paul Davies, *Are We Alone? Philosophical Implications of the Discovery of Extraterrestrial Life*. New York: Basic, 1996. An extremely thoughtful and well-written excursion into the realm of ET life and how its discovery will affect human thought and endeavors.

Steven J. Dick, *Life on Other Worlds*. New York: Cambridge University Press, 1998. A well-written overview of human preoccupation with the idea of extraterrestrial beings and the possibilities that such beings exist.

John W. Macvey, *Interstellar Travel: Past, Present, and Future*. Bath, UK: Scarborough House, 1991. A mind-bending excursion into the possibilities of journeys to the stars and technologies that might be used.

Clifford Pickover, *The Science of Aliens*. New York: Basic, 1999. A fact-filled, imaginative, and fascinating discussion of alien life and the possible physical forms it could take.

Alan E. Rubin, *Disturbing the Solar System: Impacts, Close Encounters, and Coming Attractions*. Princeton, NJ: Princeton

University Press, 2002. An eclectic, highly informative, and entertaining book about the mysteries of outer space, including the possibility of extraterrestrial life.

Carl Sagan and I.S. Shklovskii, *Intelligent Life in the Universe.* Garden City, NY: Doubleday, 1980. Long the classic work in the genre, this somewhat scholarly book by two noted scientists is slightly dated but still very comprehensive.

Robert Shapiro, *Planetary Dreams: The Quest to Discover Life Beyond Earth.* New York: Wiley, 1999. Shapiro, a chemist and expert on DNA, explores the scientific possibilities of life developing on other worlds.

Seth Shostak, *Sharing the Universe: Perspectives on Extraterrestrial Life.* Berkeley, CA: Berkeley Hills, 1998. An excellent discussion of probable alien life, the behavior of such beings, and present efforts to contact them.

Seth Shostak and Alex Barnett, *Cosmic Company: The Search for Life in the Universe.* New York: Cambridge University Press, 2003. With one of the best texts on the subject for general readers presently available, this volume also contains many excellent photos and illustrations.

Stephen Webb, *If the Universe Is Teeming With Aliens, Where Is Everybody?* New York: Copernicus, 2002. A terrific compilation of arguments for and against the Fermi Paradox, which contends that no aliens exist because they have not yet visited Earth.

OTHER RELEVANT WORKS

BOOKS

Ben Bova and Byron Preiss, eds., *First Contact: The Search for Extraterrestrial Intelligence.* New York: New American Library, 1991.

Stuart Clark, *Life on Other Worlds and How to Find It.* London: Springer-Praxis, 2000.

Ken Croswell, *Planet Quest: The Epic Discovery of Alien Solar Systems.* New York: Free Press, 1997.

Diogenes Laertius, *Lives of Eminent Philosophers.* Trans. R.D. Hicks. 2 vols. Cambridge, MA: Harvard University Press, 1995.

Frank Drake, *Is Anyone Out There?* New York: Delacorte Press, 1992.

Fred Hoyle, *The Black Cloud.* Cutchogue, NY: Buccaneer, 1992.

Michio Kaku, *Hyperspace: A Scientific Odyssey Through Parallel Universes, Time Warps, and the 10th Dimension.* New York: Anchor, 1995.

David Koerner and Simon LeVay, *Here Be Dragons: The Scientific Quest for Extraterrestrial Life.* New York: Oxford University Press, 2000.

Lawrence M. Krauss, *The Physics of Star Trek.* New York: Harper-Collins, 1995.

Curtis Peebles, *Watch the Skies! A Chronicle of the Flying Saucer Myth.* Washington, DC: Smithsonian Institution Press, 1994.

Carl Sagan, *The Cosmic Connection: An Extraterrestrial Perspective.* New York: Dell, 1973.

———, *The Dragons of Eden.* New York: Ballantine, 1977.

Gerald A. Soffen, "Life in the Solar System," in J. Kelly Beatty et al., *The New Solar System.* Cambridge, UK: Cambridge University Press, 1999.

Kip S. Thorne, *Black Holes and Time Warps: Einstein's Outrageous Legacy.* New York: W.W. Norton, 1994.

Alfred Russel Wallace, *Man's Place in the Universe.* London: Chapman and Hall, 1904.

PERIODICALS

Tim Appenzeller, "Search for Other Earths," *National Geographic,* December 2004.

Robert Burnham, "Smallest Extrasolar Planet Found," *Astronomy,* May 2005.

Jacqueline Garget, "Mysterious Water Worlds," *Astronomy,* July 2005.

Michio Kaku, "Who Will Inherit the Universe?" *Astronomy,* February 2002.

Alan Longstaff, "Quest for a Living Universe," *Astronomy,* April 2005.

Dana Mackenzie, "Is There Life Under the Ice?" *Astronomy,* August 2001.

Alan M. MacRobert and Joshua Roth, "The Planet of 51 Pegasi," *Sky and Telescope,* January 1996.

Tahirih Motazedian, "Does Mars Have Flowing Water?" *Astronomy*, June 2004.

Robert Naeye, "Astronomers Probe Alien Skies," *Astronomy*, March 2002.

———, "An Ocean for Ganymede, Too," *Astronomy*, May 2001.

Robert Pappalardo, "Jupiter's Water Worlds," *Astronomy*, July 2004.

Carl Sagan and Frank Drake, "The Search for Extraterrestrial Intelligence," *Scientific American*, May 1975.

Seth Shostak, "Listening for a Whisper," *Astronomy*, September 2004.

Richard Talcott, "An Ice Moon Revealed," *Astronomy*, July 2005.

———, "Search for Earth-like Planets Narrows," *Astronomy*, February 2002.

Robert Zimmerman, "Seeking Other Earths," *Astronomy*, August 2004.

Internet Sources

Christopher B. Jones, "Life as We Don't Know It (Part 1)," June 2000. www.suite101.com/article.cfm/sf_and_society/44271.

J.R. Mooneyham, "The Rise and Fall of Star-Faring Civilizations in Our Own Galaxy," October 2002. http://kurellian.tripod.com/ctcta.html.

NASA, "The Center for SETI Research," 2005. www.seti.org.

NASA, "Life on Other Planets in the Solar System," updated regularly. www.resa.net/nasa/xlife_intro.htm.

Jean Schneider, "Extrasolar Planet Searches," 2005. http://cfa-www.harvard.edu/planets/searches.html.

Charles S. Tritt, "Possibilities of Life on Europa," November 2002. http://people.msoe.edu/~tritt/sf/europa.life.html.

INDEX

PICTURE CREDITS

Cover: © Peter Power/ZUMA/CORBIS

ABOUT THE AUTHOR

In addition to his acclaimed volumes on ancient civilizations, historian Don Nardo has published several studies of modern scientific discoveries and phenomena. Among these are *Black Holes*, *Comets and Asteroids*, *The Extinction of the Dinosaurs*, *Cloning*, volumes about Pluto, Neptune, and the Moon, and a biography of the noted scientist Charles Darwin. Mr. Nardo lives with his wife, Christine, in Massachusetts.